Healing Your Inner Child

Overcome Childhood Trauma, Reclaim Your Power, Build Self-Love, and Create Lasting Emotional Freedom

Avery Sage

Copyright © 2025 by Avery Sage

All rights reserved.

No portion of this book may be reproduced in any form without written permission from the publisher or author, except as permitted by U.S. copyright law.

Contents

About the Author   1

Introduction   2
Healing Your Inner Child
   Why Healing Your Inner Child is Vital
   The Inner Child and Your Emotional Blueprint

1. Recognizing Your Inner Child   5
   Introducing a New Framework for Healing
   Case Study: Jemine
   Meeting and Connecting With Your Inner Child
   A Call From Your Inner Child to Pay Attention
   Case Study: Pete
   Childhood Memories as a Map
   Staying Present While Rewinding Time
   Separating the Joy From the Pain
   Navigate Your Story
   Breaking the Silence Within
   Uncovering Feelings by Putting Pen to Paper
   Guided Visualization: Your Inner Child Awaits You

2. Breaking Free from the Past 17
   Recognizing Emotional Baggage
   Limiting Patterns Caused By Trauma
   Emotional Triggers and Childhood Experiences
   Case Study: Jen
   Rewriting Your Story
   Case Study: Bryan
   Forgiving and Letting Go
   A Groundbreaking View Into Forgiveness

3. Building Emotional Safety 26
   Understanding Emotional Triggers
   Mapping Your Triggers
   Creating Safe Spaces
   Tools of Kindness
   Case Study: Brie
   Practicing Self-Compassion
   Case Study: Rose

4. Reconnecting with Your Inner Child 34
   Meeting Your Inner Child
   Case Study: Ruth
   Listening to What Your Inner Child Needs
   Inner Child Communication Exercises
   Building a Relationship with Your Inner Child
   Maintaining a Daily Connection
   Case Study: Robert

5. Reparenting Yourself 44
   Daily Practices to Reparent
   Case Study: Hannah
   Emotional Regulation Techniques

6. Cultivating Self-Love　52
    Understanding Self-Love

    Combat Your Inner Critic
    Practicing Gratitude and Joy
    Case Study: Ben

7. Establishing Healthy Boundaries　60
    Recognizing Boundary Issues
    Case Study: Mark
    Steps to Build Strong Boundaries

8. Discovering Once Lost Joy　65
    Play and Healing: Hand in Hand
    Case Study: Michael
    Creating a Life You Love

9. Sustaining Emotional Freedom　71

    Avoiding Relapse
    The Plan For Recovery
    Case Study: Jessica
    Compassion and Confidence
    Case Study: Iris
    A Balanced Life Begins With You
    Case Study: Ava

10. Transforming Pain Into Power　79
    The Gift of a Challenging Childhood
    Living Authentically

Conclusion　84
    A Life Reclaimed

Please Leave A Review	86
References	87

About the Author

Avery Sage draws from her own transformative journey and professional expertise in trauma recovery to guide readers with wisdom, empathy, and hope. Her approach blends science, experience, and a deep understanding of what it takes to reclaim one's power and joy.

A compassionate guide and storyteller, Avery Sage has spent years exploring the transformative journey of inner healing and self-love. With a unique blend of personal experience, deep introspection, and insights hours of research and self-practice. Avery empowers readers to reconnect with their authentic selves. Through her relatable stories, practical tools, and heartfelt guidance, Avery helps individuals uncover the power of their inner child to create a life filled with joy, freedom, and emotional well-being.

Believing that healing is a deeply personal and empowering process, Avery brings a voice of empathy, encouragement, and unwavering support to readers embarking on their own journeys of transformation. Her mission is simple: to help others embrace their worth, rewrite their stories, and thrive in their emotional freedom.

Introduction

HEALING YOUR INNER CHILD

Why Healing Your Inner Child is Vital

> *Warmth is the vital element for the growing plant, and for the soul of the child.*
>
> —Carl Jung

The Inner Child and Your Emotional Blueprint

I woke up one morning several years ago to a text from a friend who I will call Tom, wishing he could change his job. *"I'm so unhappy,"* he was saying to me. *"I wish I could do something completely different."*

I thought for a moment, *What's stopping you? Go get the life you want!*

We met for coffee, and Tom told me how he doesn't believe he is able to switch career paths. He thought it was too late. Tom can be a little dramatic like that. He told me that he didn't want to "trouble his wife with uncertainty."

After some gentle soul digging by me, it became painfully obvious that Tom hadn't had choices as a child. He grew up in a house where rules were rigid, and his emotional needs were neglected. Tom was told to "grow up" when he would complain about being denied being able to follow his dreams, or want to play imaginary games. He learned that the only way to get by was to get *on*.

Without realizing it, his parents had had a strong hand in shutting down his inner child, who craved being able to explore, be curious, and find joy (although he might tell you that he still enjoyed sneaking into the cookie jar for regular midnight snacks). And now, as a married man, he *still* carries those learned beliefs (and cookies) around with him. Those beliefs inhibit his chances of progressing toward a real goal or dream.

I wondered for a long time how many Toms there are in the world today. How many people, regardless of their walk of life, *still* listen to that authoritative voice that once managed them as a child?

The quote at the start of this introduction is from Carl Jung, the original coiner of the phrase *"inner child."* As a psychologist, he worked to explore the idea that there is a part of us—every single one of us—that is innate, unique, and ever-present. It's there, whether we are consciously aware of it or not, and it wants to be seen and heard. When we lose sight of it, we lose sight of the crucial splash of color we need in life to remain connected to our creativity, playfulness, and spontaneity.

Jung was right with his quote. A child needs warmth and love, understanding and encouragement to grow, the same way a plant does. If we can water a plant, put it in direct sunlight, and re-pot it* as it grows to give it more room, why can't we do this with our inner child, too?

*(Please don't plant your children in pots. I've tried. It doesn't work.)

Inner Child Wounds

So where does that inner child go, when it's told at a young age to go away? It hides in the deepest part of us, and continues to be neglected. It longs to be seen and heard, and given a voice to express itself, but it can't.

Soon enough, the inner child becomes wounded, and you will recognize those wounds anytime you are feeling "not good enough." Whether it be in work, love, friendships, or life in general, if you feel you don't measure up, opportunities will close down for you. As they do, that will reinforce your *low self-esteem*, another wound. Verbal wounds then also creep in and add to the problems when people tell you that you weren't their first choice, that you should "tone it down," etc.

It's not uncommon in adulthood to lose yourself in feelings of guilt for things that happened to you as a child. Maybe you were constantly blamed or criticized when you were young, and you still carry that weight with you now. Why? It's not your weight to carry. Could you control the way you were treated back then? *No.* Can you control it now? *Yes.*

The problem lies with the fact that too many people believe they *can't* control their lives now. That's not your fault; this comes from the lack of belief that was taught to you, which is all about to change.

Why Trauma Doesn't Stay in the Past

The first thing we need to do is delve into the concept of trauma, and what that means for you. Trauma is broadly defined as any distressing event, which means sometimes very different things depending on the situation. Emotional neglect in childhood, for example, is considered to be a form of trauma. If your needs aren't met at a time where all your experiences, thoughts, emotions, beliefs, and connections are forming, your soul will be left with holes in it.

These holes will cause pain until they are healed, and that pain is usually tied to triggers. Triggers invite themselves into your life whenever something reminds you of a time in your past you felt mistreated. They represent unresolved trauma; and since memories are stored in the brain, trauma *freezes* your memories, making them seemingly impossible to forget or heal.

Scientifically speaking, your brain is more than capable of healing and forming new connections that strengthen you, meaning your trauma can be weakened. The changing and adapting that your brain is capable of is what I want to tap into through this book, giving you permission to focus on *real change*.

You Are Your Own Healer

I don't say that lightly. In fact, I say it with such vigor that I want you to feel it vibrate in your chest, like you're on stage at the opera. I want to bring you to life from the inside, and offer you a hand to hold as you figure out ways to feel newly empowered.

Like anything in life, we all work differently and at our own pace, and I want you to know how acceptable that is. In fact, I want you to give yourself permission to work in ways that specifically suit you, and keep you from giving up. This is not a sprint (luckily for me, who has only ever ran once—away from a raccoon, if you must know).

To achieve something incredible, you must embark on a path that is as exciting as it is necessary. Does that invoke feelings of uncertainty within? Well, anything new *does*. That doesn't mean you shouldn't walk that path. Healing is achievable, and I am proof of that. Because *I* am Tom.

CHAPTER ONE
Recognizing Your Inner Child

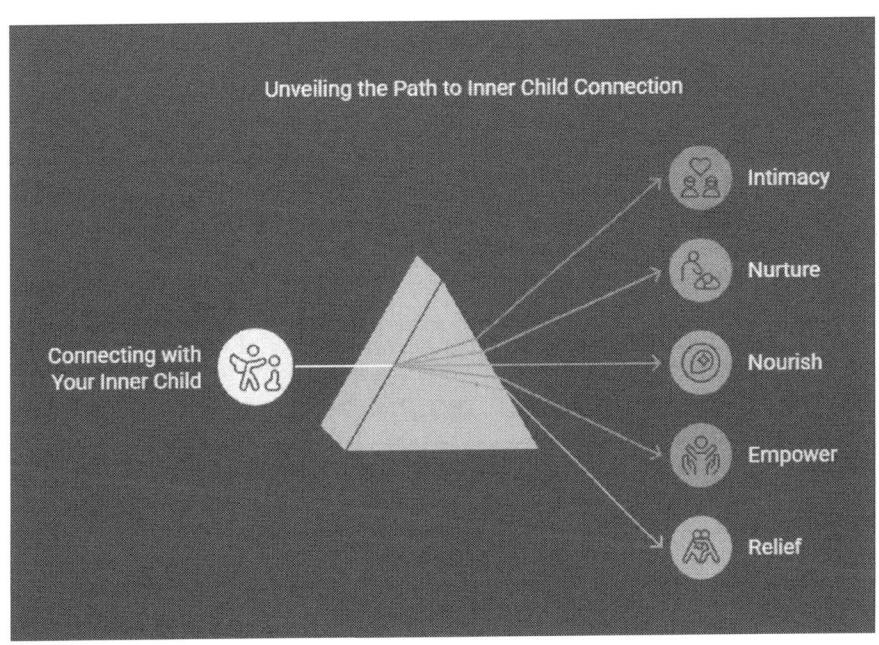

Do you see a little bit of my experiences inside your own? If you do, you will understand what it's like to be totally unaware that healing your inner child is the answer to changing your life. All those hopes and dreams you have for yourself, or even just *letting go* of everything you went through, is achievable for everybody with a little work.

Your inner child lives inside of you, whether you've met them before or not. They've walked your path, witnessed every day of your life, and influence your thoughts and feelings along the way. Now is the time to begin to recognize who they are in a way you've never experienced before.

Introducing a New Framework for Healing

You've seen books that ooze science from beginning to end, and you've likely fanned through titles that are as deep as they are negative. This is not the first book that discusses inner-child healing. It *is, however*, one of the only books that positively picks out *exactly* what you need in order to start your healing journey.

I want this book to be a pocket of hope you can always refer to. I want it to be a hand for you to hold. My approaches come from a unique blend of research studies, as well as my own experience and knowledge in the realm of healing and trauma.

Life is not black or white. Healing is not linear. Trauma is not the same for us all. Personalities differ. None of us are the same! That's what makes the world such a vibrant place. We need to find our *own* path, and not be led by somebody who is either going to slow you down, swamp you with heavy ideas, or want you to move faster than you're able to.

There is no final exam for healing your inner child, but there *is* opportunity, from looking at new ways to connect with your inner child, to combining past theories with my own techniques and tools for healing. I *promise* you will find new ways to rewrite your story and frame your past. In doing so, you will be offered ways to let go and forgive. You can learn to love yourself, and be proud of who you are and what you went through. I guarantee your self-worth will grow to a point where you finally feel like your authentic self.

As an added bonus, you can finally build boundaries around yourself, and learn what you are no longer willing to accept. (Move over, everybody!) That will bring joy to a heart that has lacked it for some time, brought to you by your very own inner child. This is a transformational time, and it is my promise to you that you will *remain* transformed. Think of it as a gift you don't need to keep the receipt for.

Case Study: Jemine

I want to start by offering you a story by somebody who wrote to me last year about the first time she met her inner child. Jemine is one of the most skeptical people I know, which was why I was surprised with her account. Here is her letter.

I have been hard on myself since forever. Nothing was ever good enough. I hated the thought of letting go and having too much fun because I thought it would only be a matter of time before somebody told me to stop it, or calm down, or grow up.

I didn't think I had an inner child. It's a bit like Santa—I just didn't believe something like that could exist. It seemed silly to try and find the child I used to be, and find ways to comfort her and let her know I had found her and she was no longer lost.

As I have always been a fan of drawing, I bought a new sketchpad and some color pens one day to try and resurrect a hobby. I didn't even think about inner-child work until I started to draw, and those drawings all seemed to circle around the same theme—my childhood home. I'd draw my house, my room growing up, the garden with the swing by the porch; everything came back to life.

Soon enough, she was there; the old me, or should I say the "young" me. I didn't see her before me, I felt her. I felt like I was seven again, drawing and feeling like it was the only thing in the world worth doing.

If I can be completely honest, it felt like reuniting with an old soulmate. I'm a woman who comes from a strict religious background, so I am used to trying to put all my focus on my God in times of pain, which helps in ways I cannot describe. That moment I was mind-to-mind, heart-to-heart with my inner child gave me the chance to look into myself and realize she was there all along. I realized that she needed me, and that I needed her, too.

Personally for me—and it won't be the same for everybody—but I felt like my path of religion encouraged me to this moment, and I thank God I was able to meet my inner child. We meet up several times a week, and each time we do, she lets me be and feel that little more free—the way we should all feel.

Meeting and Connecting With Your Inner Child

Your inner child has been crying out for you to meet them. The good news is that it's never too late to reunite with the innocent part of you that forever lives on!

One of the main takeaway messages from meeting your inner child is to learn how to be less hard on yourself, and much more compassionate. Life is hard! I can't say that enough. We all face challenges; some we overcome easily, while others are harder to navigate. Your dream might be to be your own boss, but your lack of confidence in your abilities is preventing you from taking the leap.

The question I've got for you is this: What is stopping you? I'm not talking about finances; I'm asking you what's going on in your mind. When you think about being successful, what's really stopping you?

I want you to stop thinking about the excuses, and start getting excited for that connection. What might that feel like for you? I want to remove the "*inner*" from "inner child," and show you what it feels like when you initially connect with yours. Ironically, that process can be summed up by the acronym I.N.N.E.R.:

I: Intimacy. This is about as deep and personal as you can get with yourself, and I don't want you to underestimate that at all. If that feels uncomfortable to you initially, stick with it. It won't always feel that way, trust me.

N: Nurture. There's a lot of making up to do, right? That love you have lacked can now be given to you and channeled through your inner child.

N: Nourish. Enrichment time! Now you get to start to explore the fun things you have been isolated from, the joyous feelings your inner child has been longing for your adult self to experience.

E: Empower. What's more empowering than taking charge of your well-being? What could provide you with more power than recognizing where other people went wrong, and how that wrongfulness affected you? Rewriting your own history starts with one decision, and meeting your child is *that*.

R: Relief. It feels relieving to release the weights that have kept your spirit down all this time. Meeting your inner child is how you start to find peace, and work it into every aspect of your life.

Creating a series of meetings for connecting with your inner child will help you find your way through your own connection. Once that meeting has taken place, you might wonder what comes next for you in your journey. What does your inner child want you to start paying more attention to?

A Call From Your Inner Child to Pay Attention

Despite our different traumas, experiences, and reasons for wanting to reach out to our inner child for healing, the sentiment they individually offer each of us is the same. If I could paraphrase that for you based on what I know and have felt, it is this:

Hi, it's me. Do you remember me?

You might recall snippets of time we spent together, or you may have real trouble thinking back that far. Don't worry—I'm not saying you're old! But I am implying that so much time has passed. What have you done with it? I've had to watch you carry pain around with you. I wish you would have reached me sooner, but the important thing is that you're here now.

I know you better than anybody, because you're me. I know you struggle with self-acceptance, and that you wish you were more resilient. I know your anxiety and sadness can take over at times, and stop you from doing what really makes you happy. It's trapped you for too long, and so I'm here, calling out to you to pay attention to those unhealed parts of you.

If you want to know a secret, it's that there is joy to be found where fear currently lives. Remember when you used to love having fun, and suddenly it all stopped?

This is your call to action. To tend to me, to tend to the damage caused by others, to tend to you now. The love you need can come from you, and I can help you find it.

Love,

Me

How do you feel reading that? Does it hit home? For me, it's a pretty universal realization that there's a lot of pain out there that can be fixed by responding. And by the way, feel free to reply to that letter as if it were your own inner child talking directly to you, and you alone! I did, and that's what pointed me to open wounds of the soul that needed my immediate attention.

CASE STUDY: PETE

Pete did this too, only instead of a letter, it was a different sensory experience that created a surprise discovery when he *least expected it*. Pete's story hit my chest like a hammer on a block of ice. I would be doing both him and a lot of *you* a disservice if I failed to offer him this book as a platform for retelling it.

I was four years old when my dad left home. At 39, I've still not seen nor heard from him since, so that tells me everything I need to know about him.

When he left, my mom sank into a world of her own, and forgot I existed. Before he left, she wasn't much better, as all I remember her doing was locking herself away with my dad for hours. I'd be hungry, tired, cold; nothing made her prioritize me. I began to get used to it, and when I was able to, I'd start making myself peanut butter sandwiches (as best as any older toddler could, anyway). I lived off those for what seemed like forever. If I felt sad, I had to push it to the back of my mind and try to just survive.

It wasn't long before she started drinking heavily. Without him, it was like she needed a replacement addiction. I was made to feel as if I was in the way, and never given the love, care or attention any child needed. These are what I deem basic human rights. There was never money for the heat to go on, so I spent a lot of time sitting in my winter coat in my house while my mom drank away the money to keep us warm.

I grew into somebody who was overly self-sufficient, relying on and trusting nobody else to play that role for me. I felt so alone, but it was all I knew.

I had no idea the amount of pain I was carrying with me until I found an old stuffed animal I used to cuddle at night as a child. I smelt it, and that musty aroma threw me right back to being four years old again. I saw myself in that house; cold, hungry and alone.

That was the most painful experience of my life, but that pain became the catalyst for regular inner-child work.

How does Pete's story sit with you? Have you locked away your trauma all these years? I can help you find the key as we start to now untangle your childhood memories, and map them out.

Childhood Memories as a Map

When it comes to maps, never hand me one. I am probably the *worst* map reader in the world. Once I got lost trying to find my way *out* of a national park, even with a map *and directions.*

Our childhood can make us feel equally as lost sometimes, especially when we're trying to work through so much sadness and pain that happened a long time ago. You'll see on your own map landscapes of joy, followed by haunted houses present with shadowy corners of pain. It's a tough part of your healing journey to navigate, but that shouldn't mean you give up. Giving up will put you right back to where you started, and that's evidently where you don't want to remain.

This chapter balances your curiosity with a healthy dollop of self-care along the way. Visiting your past can feel like entering a time machine; but there are tools to help you and ways to cope. You're in the right place to learn them all.

Staying Present While Rewinding Time

I went to a movie theater recently and watched the latest Pixar film. (I alone skewed the average age of the audience by at least twenty-five years.) I sat back and watched the movie in its entirety; then when it ended, I got up, walked out, and got on with my life.

That is how I want you to explore the past.

Your childhood has come and gone, and what happened (both good and bad) made you who you are today. Reflecting should be a way for you to gain insight without being physically or mentally drawn back to a time that made you unhappy. Choosing to sit and watch your past as if it were a movie that you can separate yourself from is the ideal way to produce results without lingering pain overtaking your purpose to heal.

When your memories return, not *all* of them will be bad if you look hard enough. Separating the good from the bad is how you start to win at mapping your childhood out.

Separating the Joy From the Pain

The neural pathways that process both pain *and* joy *both* derive from the same regions of your brain, called the *amygdala,* and in that region sits the *pallidum,* and the *nucleus accumbens*. The pallidum is stimulated by pain, and the nucleus accumbens becomes active when a person perceives pleasure. This makes the amygdala as a whole the *desire center*; wanting to avoid pain, and wanting to seek that pleasure.

Because of these areas being so close together in the brain, parts of the neural pathways between pleasure and pain overlap. As the ratios of pleasure and pain change, so does your perception and what those perceptions are associated with. In other words, if you have a problem, it can become *more* of a problem if you are also under another cloud of stress at that time. Shifting your focus to something more positive can *alleviate* those issues, lessening the use of the pain center part of your brain.

Experiencing positivity is only dependent on how able we are to process, regulate, and identify the negative. Separating joy from pain is necessary for emotional boundaries and gaining a deeper level of understanding ourselves.

Joy and pain can live separately within us, and we can honor each emotion as or when needed; it's possible! How? *Acceptance.* That's right. No shiny bows needed for this one!

Separating sadness from happiness is only possible if you accept the sad exists, allowing it the space it needs in order to be validated. Feel it. Allow it. Be sad if you need to be, but equally when you discover a joyful memory, you need to absorb it as richly as you do the sad. In fact, giving yourself permission to feel sad can be joyous within itself, almost relieving! (Now you are beginning to bring the R of I.N.N.E.R. to life.)

Navigate Your Story

Now that you've learned how to separate joy from pain, how can you actively explore the story of you? Being able to be open and honest with how your memories affect your emotions will help you look deeper into your story, and how it has been written.

The story of your life began the day you were born, and it has taken many twists and turns along the way. Has your narrative made you feel like the victim or the victor? The stories you tell yourself are the stories you also tell others. I want to walk you through exploring those crucial first few chapters of your story using *narrative therapy* practices by Michael White and David Epston, but in an updated and more specific way to suit you. This is in three steps.

1. Externalize

Let's go back to that movie theater I mentioned before, where we talked about the idea that your past can be what you look back *on*, not fall back *in*. This means you can view what you've labeled your narrative, and see it for what it is. Sometimes, yes, that can mean admitting you've used your trauma as a way to escape your life *now*.

2. Pull Apart One Event

Or if you want to look at it another way: dig deep. Here is where you think about your childhood and how it was written out for you, how you really didn't get any say as a small child. Instead of saying, "I felt neglected as a child" and leaving it at that, you might want to go a layer deeper. *In what ways were you neglected? How old were you?* Think of one time you were neglected, and work through it in detail. What this does is sweep away general feelings of neglect, and get to the root of the problem. Sometimes that can look like:

I had a parent who worked long hours and was never home

I had a parent with addictions

My parents had severe mental health issues

This isn't about making excuses for the people who were supposed to care for you; this is taking what happened and reframing it. The foundation of your stress was somebody else's poor choices.

3. Tell Your Story

In the search for meaning, you will find your story being told. That's where your purpose lies. When you can look for purpose, you can retell your story in a way that feels more healing. I will give you a brief example.

Natalie was abused by her father through all her childhood and into her twenties. Eventually, she began to associate all her fears with the limitations imposed upon her, and all the ways her father used to criticize, ridicule, and control her. Natalie broke contact with her father in order to not receive this abuse any longer. When she did, she felt anger for several years toward him. This did nothing for her healing.

Eventually, Natalie began to see the real problem: that her father had mental health issues that went beyond his abuse aimed at her. It wasn't her fault, yet all this time she felt shackled to the concept that she was a terrible person who deserved terrible treatment.

In telling her story to herself, she laid down new paths of hope, knowing that her lack of contact could now open doors, instead of keeping them wedged firmly shut. It was a narrative that needed tweaking, and in doing so, Natalie was able to shift herself from a victim to a survivor.

Natalie's story speaks for many who struggle with overcoming abuse in childhood. As the survivor in her emerged, so did her inner child. But does that shift come easy for everybody? No, it doesn't. Let's look at ways you can add sound to the silence in your soul.

Breaking the Silence Within

I'm always drawn to research from Californian therapist *Kim Egel* when I think about the struggles people have with reaching out to their inner child. I've heard account after account of people just staring at their friends, family, or therapist with a blank face, saying things like:

"I don't even know where to start."

"I've tried, but nothing happens or works."

"I'm beginning to think I don't even have an inner child."

If this sounds like you, I want you to pause for a moment and take a breath. You see, Egel believes that any kind of resistance, or a lack of believing in your inner child, will inhibit the way you reunite with them. Any kind of emotional frustration will only create a barrier between you both, and I think that's a key point to remember when you're feeling nothing but silence within.

You're not going to hear a knock at the door and see your inner child (wouldn't that be slightly freaky if you did?), but you *will* feel what I call an *inner notification*. Inner notifications can take such forms as:

A breakthrough, with your emotions shifting as you make progress.

A sudden, lighter feeling, like relief.

An insight into your childhood.

A memory that arises out of nowhere.

An overwhelming desire to protect your inner child.

These are all signs an inner notification has reached you, and signs that you are making headway with finding your inner child. Below, I describe two exercises that are proven to encourage receiving an inner notification.

Uncovering Feelings by Putting Pen to Paper

Journaling sounds like a lot of fun if you enjoy it, or are used to picking up a pen and writing. For others, it doesn't come as naturally. When you're specifically looking to get something out of journaling, the pressure can seem even more, which is why I have created five journal prompts for you to uncover suppressed feelings you may have.

The Letter That Was Never Sent. We never willingly want our inner child to just disappear. Children are hard-wired to want to have fun, splash in puddles, roll in mud, sing and dance like nobody's watching, and be totally carefree. It's only taken away by people who want those parts of us to be suppressed. So, whoever that person was for you, I want you to write them a letter that will never get sent. The idea is to let your words flow without self-censorship. And hey, you're an adult; you can swear if you want to! Write down any truths you've held back. Write *why* you held them back, how they made you feel, and what's been missing from your life as a result. The one and only rule you have is to *never send the letter.*

Conversations With Your Shadow Self. Your shadow self is the part of you that keeps hold of all the emotions you are avoiding. It's time to converse with it! A dialogue is a simple way to start. You can begin by asking them, "What are you trying to tell me?" Let that part of you respond, in any way it happens to flow out. The key is *noticing* how it flows. Is that shadow part of you happy? Sad? Rude?

Emotional Time-Hop. When was the last time you had an overwhelming emotion but you didn't express it, fully or at all? I want you to write where you were at the time, and who you were with. What was the emotion? What prevented you from letting it out and expressing it? Imagine this was you as a child. What would you say to your younger self?

Isle of Emotional Discovery. You're on a gorgeous island, surrounded by deep, yet clear blue seas (thanks for the invite...). On the sandy shores around you are scattered emotions that belong to you. They're washing up in real time! What do you see? Shapes, colors, sizes, textures—they all matter and add detail to this process. Pick an object up and ask it where it came from. Imagine that it can talk back to you, and write down what you're getting from it. This exercise can *wildly* open up your emotional doors, and lead you to answers you never even considered.

Dig to Explore. Lastly, digging to explore is a fun way to visualize your emotions rising to the surface. You're an emotional archeologist! Instead of digging up old bones or coins from thousands of years ago, I want you to dig up emotions you've kept hidden. With each discovery, I want you to write what that emotion looks like, or its shape or size. Going deeper (no pun intended), I want you to think about *why* it was buried in the first place. Again, this tool is to help you *visualize* your emotions, rather than simply try to *feel* them, which can be difficult for a lot of people.

Guided Visualization: Your Inner Child Awaits You

Now, let's take a look at visualizing meeting your inner child, and how you can start practicing today. It can be tricky to visualize something specific. When I first started trying to meet my inner child, it didn't happen on the first (or second, or third, or even fourth!) try. I even laughed aloud at myself one time when I was in the shower singing "*God Only Knows*" (one of my favorite childhood songs, and no, I am not showing my age...) to try to find my younger self.

Instead of asking you to also sound like cats fighting, I want you to turn to your imagination. Start with the most obvious: closing your eyes and taking a deep breath in. You want to get into the zone. Where is a place that brings you peace? The beach? A forest? A field of flowers? Picture yourself there, in whatever weather opens your heart. The air is fresh, and the sound of the waves or trees ignite your senses, helping you see a clearing bathed in golden light before you.

Right in the center sits a wooden bench. Sitting upon it and waiting patiently is a younger version of you. Picturing them there already is a great way of instigating meeting your inner child. Now I want you to notice their posture. What are they expressing to you? How are they looking at you? Are they shy? Maybe they're curious as to why you're suddenly there. Pause just a few steps away to take in what you see. How do you feel now you see them?

Only when you feel ready to do so, walk closer. Kneel down so you can look right into their eyes, and smile gently. You must at this point want to say something—what will it be? Whatever comes up, go with it. This is your safe space where nobody else is invited. It's for you to be honest, open and let the love and healing start to flow.

Analyzing the silence is an affirming place to land, because then you can start to really view your past for what it is: something you can break free from. That's exactly where we are going next.

Chapter Two

Breaking Free from the Past

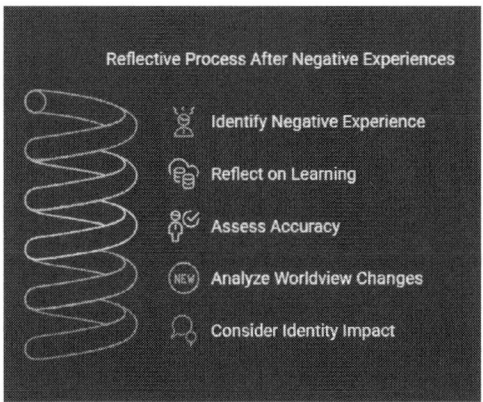

The past need not be your prison. This is not a place where you will get locked up each night for bedtime. The past is a memory, and yes, those memories are not *all* positive. Making the mistake of believing you are trapped in the past, however, will keep the past alive.

Nobody wants to live their lives stuck in painful memories. It's time to break free. The first step to that is recognizing what you've been carrying with you all this time, and I don't mean your grocery bags from the farmer's market.

Recognizing Emotional Baggage

Emotional baggage may be a term familiar to you. It means carrying any unfinished issues around with you. Stress, pain, and trauma is weighing your spirit down to the point where it affects you and your relationships. When you feel heaviness in your body but you're *not* sick, it usually points at emotional baggage trapped inside you, and in turn, the limiting patterns that weight creates over time.

Limiting Patterns Caused by Trauma

Imagine you have a rotten apple in your bag that you forgot was there. Every morning, you put a new apple in your bag to take to work, but by the time you get there, it's already started to rot too, as it was placed next to your forgotten older one. Every day this happens, and you get frustrated. You just want to enjoy a nice apple on your lunch break, but it's proving impossible.

Your limiting patterns are that rotten apple—and any new apple is the potential for you to be happy again, whether that's a new relationship, a job offer, or an evening out with friends. While the rotten apple remains, that rot will spread.

Limiting patterns are caused by unprocessed trauma; and like the apple above, you may not even realize it's there, but rather just becomes a part of your life. What this can do is attract the wrong thoughts, peoples, beliefs, or opinions to you, rather than those that will do you good.

Unprocessed trauma affects your limiting patterns in five ways:

Making You Conditioned to the Chaos. Your chaotic past was *not* normal! There are too many people who become accustomed to the unpredictability of their earlier years, and they take it with them in their adult lives.

All-or-Nothing Thinking. You don't have to protect yourself by thinking in such extreme ways, but this is what happens when traumatic events play a part in creating negative cognitive distortions. These are thoughts you might have that aren't based on reality or any kind of fact, essentially *assuming the worst about every situation.*

Self-Sabotaging. How many times have you thrown water over any passion you try to set alight in your life? You don't feel worthy of it, so you ruin it. Your trauma has taught you to think that you are either going to be abandoned eventually, or that something won't work out. This is truly limiting, and by default, you will prove your limiting beliefs to be right.

Constantly Being on the Go. Being constantly on the go, and *never* stopping even when tired, is a common flight response. The need to outrun or escape from something is usually the main reason why people don't like to do *nothing*, and is linked to overachieving or needing their routines to be perfect.

Awakening the Inner Critic. Breaking news: You don't have to believe every thought you have! Trauma can leave a heavy stamp, can't it? That voice inside your head telling you that you can't do this, or you can't achieve that, will disempower you. The reason the voice exists is because it aligns with your strong feelings of low self-worth, and that acts to fuel your inner critic, which in turn fuels your lack of self-worth. It's a vicious cycle!

Emotional Triggers and Childhood Experiences

With so many ways to limit your beliefs, what can trigger you into these limiting thoughts, and where do they start? Adverse childhood experiences (ACEs) needs a whole book to itself, but I want to give you the main meaning behind it.

If you grow up in a home that wasn't loving, nurturing or stable, you will have experienced some kind of adversity. These experiences mean you lack the happiness and good health to grow the way you deserve. Just one ACE increases your probability of experiencing another; and the more you have, the more emotionally dysregulated you will become.

What can trigger your ACEs in adulthood can be moments when you feel:

- Abandoned
- Trapped in some kind of conflict
- Ignored, or like you don't matter
- Sad
- Angry
- Like you need help
- Shame
- Anxiety

The specific list depends on you as an individual and how you respond to triggers. It's a complex ball of wool to untangle, but you *can* do it. Just like Jen did.

Case Study: Jen

I was taught that the only way to do something properly was to do it perfectly. If my homework wasn't to my parents' standards, I had to do it all over again. If I made my bed, I had to fold the corners properly, or they would pull the blanket back and tell me to start again. Everything I did was pulled apart, despite trying my best.

When I was 18, I left home for college, and I never returned after that. I met a boy my age and we fell in love, and he was one of the first people to tell me that I didn't have to try to be perfect, because nobody is. He noticed all the ways I kept trying to make everything just right. In the end, what he said to me changed my life: "Have you ever thought that your parents' obsession with wanting you to be perfect was in fact their own imperfections projected onto you?"

Mind. Blown. I began to see my own space as a place I could be myself, and over time I felt better about just making my bed, without the folded corners!

Rewriting Your Story

Does it sound intimidating to rewrite your story? Are you currently sighing deeply under the incorrect assumption that rewriting it just *isn't* possible? Well, I'm happy to break it to you that you can!

Challenging Negative Core Beliefs: Step by Step

I am not enough.

I can't do it.

I am nothing but a burden.

I don't fit in.

Nobody likes me.

Sound familiar? I hope not; but I have a feeling at least some of this will resonate with you. These are negative core beliefs that you believe about yourself. They may sound like fleeting comments in passing, but they are deeply ingrained into your character—and they *prevent you* from being the amazing person that you are.

Negative core beliefs develop when we are young, and they are reinforced by our environment. The only way you can change them is by acknowledging they are there. The challenge is to understand this goes beyond just trying to think "logically." Don't feel daunted about diving into your emotions—just grab your goggles and jump in!

Thought diaries are a great way to identify specific core beliefs. This might look like:

- About me: "I am a failure"
- About others: "People are unkind"
- About the world: "The future looks bleak"
- Anything else: "Exercise is useless"

Notice patterns. What negative beliefs are you holding onto? Once you have identified them, you can now challenge them. It's time to disagree with yourself! Remember here that core beliefs are the emotional equivalent of body builders; they're *strong*. You can do it.

First, take a core belief you have about yourself; let's use the example above, that you're a failure. Rate that belief out of ten. It'll likely be high, so let's say 8 here. The challenge is to write down any evidence to the contrary of the belief that you're a failure. You might write:

I have a job that allows me to pay my bills and have fun.

I have a college degree.

I have lovely friends.

I passed my driving test.

I changed a light bulb last week.

I grew vegetables in my garden last summer.

When I was 12, I won a writing competition.

It doesn't matter what you write, as long as it argues against the belief that you're a failure. It's important to come to a point of understanding that just because some things don't work out, it doesn't make you an automatic failure. If that were the case, then heaven help us all! It's time to be realistic, not negative.

Reframing

The kind of work described above is known as *reframing*. Your past, present, and future can all be seen in your mind right now, but the only one of those to actually exist is the present. If you can change the narrative of your past, you can change what your present and future look like.

Reframing your past has *five crucial steps* to it, so let's get deeper into them, one by one.

1. List an experience you've had that has negatively impacted your life.

2. Write what you learned from that experience. It doesn't matter at this point if what you learned is negative.

3. Think about what you know about that experience now, then ask, "Is this 100 percent accurate? Have I omitted or added anything due to the time between then and now?"

4. Now think about how that experience shaped you. How did it make you view the world? If you looked at the world differently afterwards, in what ways did you do so?

5. Finally, I want you to think about how that experience shaped your identity. This now puts you in a prime position to consider reshaping your identity based on you might view your experience differently. What does having been through something so difficult teach you about yourself as a person? What could that mean for your future? Is there an underlying strength involved in overcoming it?

Do you see clearly now how reframing your experiences can reframe your future? Talk about empowering! Bryan knows *all about that*.

CASE STUDY: BRYAN

My father abused me as a child. Shouting, criticizing, belittling, the odd smack here and there. It was all about control. The less he had, the angrier he got.

I grew up unhappy and hollowed out from the pain he caused me. I needed a father figure to show me how to grow into a man, but it was mostly guesswork by myself and copying my friends.

I reacted badly to a project failing at work one day, and my boss suggested I see somebody to help with my anger. I did, and soon enough he opened up these windows of discovery for me.

I came to realize that my father was abusive because he himself was abused. He came from a house with nothing in it, no possessions, no love. All he knew was how to control, because that's what he learned as a boy. Generational abuse was rife in my family the more I started to open my eyes to it. Brothers, cousins, aunts—there was always a key person who failed the kids that followed.

The most empowering thing about realizing all of this was to understand that I could control my own life and where it heads. I didn't want to repeat behavior that to me solved nothing. It took a lot of therapy and self-compassion to forgive myself for the years I didn't see the bigger picture.

My fiancé and I are expecting our first baby, a boy, in three months' time, and I have made a vow to myself to be present, to see the world through his eyes. I like to think he is going to find my inner child for me, and I can't wait.

Forgiving and Letting Go

For Bryan, there was an element of forgiveness in his story. But exactly how easy *is* it to forgive? What does forgiveness mean to you? The answer will be different for everybody. For some, it might look like simply letting somebody off the hook, but in fact forgiveness has many complex layers to it.

The research that has gone into healing proves that some people are more inclined to forgive than others. Does that sound like you? It sounds like my best friend when I turn up to lunch late, that's for sure! With the ability to forgive somebody comes the release of pent-up negative emotions such as anger and resentment. If you're forgiving by nature, you're less likely to be anxious, or exhibit depression and stress. Doesn't that sound like something we could all get on board with?

A Groundbreaking View Into Forgiveness

There are two parts to forgiveness, and most people only really focus on the first part, which is to forgive others. It's commendable to be able to allow feelings of resentment to pass enough so that you consciously forgive a person who has wronged you, but I'm not kidding when I tell you that you can do it. A lot of the time, it's simply a case of *wanting* to—and what can hold you back is remembering all the ways you were treated unfairly by them.

So, I want you to step away from forgiveness as a concept for a moment, and reroute your focus to your own expectations of the person in question. Understand that an apology may never come. You may *never* hear that person tell you how regretfully they treated you. Instead of wishing things were different, how about changing your expectations of that person? Accept that they aren't on the same level of values as you are, and adjust the way you anticipate them to be so. That doesn't mean you *weren't* wronged or mistreated, but it *does* shed a light on how different we all are.

What helps *you* forgive might not work for you, so here are three different practices you can try. Remember, there's no right or wrong way to do this.

Write Down The Benefits. We sometimes focus so hard on forgiving because it's the "right thing to do" that we forget what good it does us to forgive. Writing down the *you* who could exist after forgiveness will give you an insight into the benefits of doing so. Examples might include *"I will feel free," "I can finally work on my goals,"* or *"I can meet my inner child and comfort them."*

Think About Forgiveness Being Shown To You. This is a practice you can do when you need to understand how forgiveness feels. Again, don't think, "This person *abused* me; why should I forgive them?" You are not forgiving the abuse; you are letting go of how it made you feel. You are releasing the burden the abuse had on you. If you have been shown forgiveness, then you can be the one to show it, too.

Understand The Forgiveness Process. It takes time to practice the process of forgiveness. Most people think it's *"I forgive you, the end."* What a story that would be! Forgiveness can actually happen over and over. The key is knowing how to do it, especially if new emotions bubble up from a trigger one day. Know that small pains can be revisited, but so can the act of forgiveness.

Leaning Into Releasing Emotional Ties to the Past

Try not to feel overwhelmed about doing everything at once. There's a lot to take in, and much of that can lead you back to your past. How can your past feel easier when you do that, though? I want you to see these exercises as a way to set your ties to the past free. They're achievable if you put the work in, and I believe you can.

The Day-By-Day. This is more of a *conscious awareness* exercise, but you can do it every day. I want you to take moments every day to *remember* that your journey may take a little while, but all you have to worry about is today. Don't climb your mountain before you've got the tools; and once you acquire those tools, use them every day, even if that's to do something small.

Movement. You don't have to be Fred Astaire to experience the fact that *movement* is magical. What kind of movement is completely up to you, and that's why this exercise is pretty loose. There are a plethora of ways to move, including dance, swimming, yoga, tai chi, gardening, stretching, and many more. Believe it or not, emotions that get trapped in the body can be released when we *move with intent*. Those negative ties you have to your past are all stored as tension, muscle aches, pain, and inflammation. Certain types of somatic therapy are not only proven to work, but are also used widely now to help with releasing trauma and emotions.

Chapter Three

Building Emotional Safety

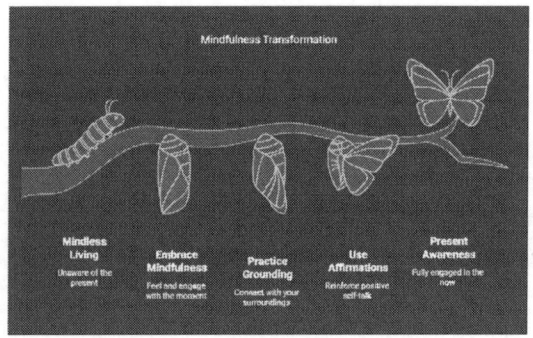

Stop for a moment right now and bring a vision of your best friend to your mind. Envisage them clearly until you start to smile to yourself and feel that friendly warmth stirring in your gut. That warmth is *exactly* what emotional safety is. They accept you for who you are, no matter who that may be, and I am *hoping* you do the same for them. My own best friend accepts me wholly, despite my scratchy singing voice and inability to be on time 95 percent of the time. We have been best friends for over fifteen years now, and I'm so thankful for them.

The magnetic pull you have toward your best friend isn't because of their looks, what color hair they have, or how big their house or car is. It's their loyalty—how they are there for you when you need them, and how freely your emotions can flow when you get together. To build those kinds of connections with someone takes time and effort, and I speak for a lot of people when I say that I don't simply trust every random person I meet. They need to earn it, and I hope they feel the same towards me, because that would mean *they* value the same things as me.

Any unresolved experience from your childhood may have the strong potential to leave you lacking in emotional safety, or even knowing what emotional safety *is*. When somebody who was supposed to be there for you fails to be, that innate, instinctive connection won't be a foundation for all others to come in your life. You wouldn't have realized it at the time, but you needed that kind of love and support. It wasn't just, "how it was back then"—it was a part of your core being that was missing.

This is where you get to build your *own* foundation now. We can refer to the past and capture what we did not get, so we can start to provide it for ourselves. I believe this is the epicenter of empowerment, and I know everybody is capable of exploring this and using it to help you heal.

Understanding Emotional Triggers

Triggers act to resurface a painful memory linked to your trauma; and believe me, they can be intense. The panic that ensues is a blend of remembering your trauma and fearing a repeat of said trauma in the present moment. This is where things can get a little messy, because you're likely *not* reliving it—you're just being reminded of it. That's still very uncomfortable, but the brain can't tell the difference. When you're in a certain situation, your mind and/or body will often let you know that there's some intense feelings going on inside you that you can't ignore.

I want to not only help you discover what your own personal triggers are, but I want to lay them down like your own official emotional map, so you can navigate your way through them to the other side. Let's do that now.

When you experience trauma, there is *no* safety present. Your body and mind want to protect you, which can result in negative behavior. You run. You freeze. You yell. You cry. You fight. Your brain scans the environment to quickly determine what to do to best help you, depending on who you are, what you're experiencing, and how your nervous system is used to operating (some people's are more sensitive than others).

It's kind of a beautiful thing when you think about it, the idea that we are such a complex system of processes and responses. But trouble can brew when we are no longer in that traumatic situation. We have moved on, yet we seem stuck, and that's how trauma constantly pulls you back to that moment. We relive trauma when something related to it reminds us of it. It might be a smell, or a color. It could be as random as a flower, or a song, or even the feeling of discomfort. As the body and brain *never* forget (after all, they want to remember the trauma to keep you safe in the future), it's common to relive your trauma as if it were happening all over again. I know how tiring that is.

When you're triggered, everything can come flooding back, and it's as if you're right there where you felt the most pain. Trauma is so personal to each and every individual that I'd never assume your own, but I *do* know reliving it can feel like a very real and very dense ball of darkness is trapped inside you.

If you want to heal, the odds are in your favor, and although it's never linear, your journey can and will free that feeling from you. In order to heal, you need to understand your own emotional triggers, where they started, and how your experiences made you this version of yourself today, reading this book. To be honest with yourself about your triggers is to take the first step into a world of emotional safety. The first step in that honesty is understanding *why* certain situations provoke such intense reactions.

Emotional Intensity

The emotional intensity you feel when you're triggered can result in a plethora of responses. And let's be real here; it's never going to be positive. To understand your triggers, you must start to unpick what you went through.

We all have an inner child, and often they're left to try to understand all by themselves. Because they're children, they can't do that. They need the mature, adult *you* to help them. This is where you can really show your strength, by facing what happened with vulnerability and tenderness.

To have such high emotional intensity to your triggers is a form of emotional dysregulation, meaning you struggle to control them at times. What's equally challenging is the fact that your mind and body are constantly fighting to keep you safe, even though the trauma itself has passed. So where does that leave you? With anxiety, depression, conflicted relationships, feelings of shame and/or anger, and the heavy assumption that you'll never move on.

We are *not* meant to feel any of these emotions on a permanent, consistent basis, and that's where we can start to see time for what it really is: *the past, the present, and the future.* The past is where your pain lies, and it's been brought with you into the present moment. Now is the time for real change, as this part of time is the only part you can control. And those intense emotions? They *can* be a thing of the past, so that your future begins to look brighter.

Mapping Your Triggers

Mapping your triggers may not sound like something you want to roll your sleeves up and jump into, but it will give you a great vantage point to view where problems started in your past. Here are some prompts below to help you get started in mapping out what happens, and why. These are the kinds of questions you have to ask yourself if you want to start to connect the dots and see what picture is created from it.

What Was My Emotion? Be honest here; don't sugarcoat things if you felt rage or uncontrolled panic.

Where Was I? Knowing where you were can give you a clue as to what kind of personal safety you felt right before you were triggered.

What Happened? Again, be honest. Don't leave anything out, because you need those small details in order to figure out what's going on.

Who Was There? An important one! Friends, family, strangers, loud people, confrontational people—think about it all, because it all matters.

How Did I Feel? From thoughts to physical feelings, you have to think about what the moment did to you as a whole.

Was It an Internal or External Trigger? Did the trigger involve a specific place or person? Maybe instead it was a moment of feeling self-critical, or leaning into your deepest insecurities.

I don't want you to write everything down only to then put the writing away. This is a moment of self-discovery that you have access to. Regularly revisit what you wrote. Over time, what you'll notice is a pattern starting to emerge. You'll be able to say, "You know what? It seems to be when this or that happens." That's where you are starting to find yourself!

Creating Safe Spaces

Safe spaces are *not* the same as comfort zones. I don't believe comfort zones are entirely healthy, because I think they are designed to keep you small even when you have that urge to grow and explore outside it. Your *safe* space is the zone where you can gather your thoughts, energy, and confidence in a way that suits and validates you. It's where you go when everything feels like too much, and where time to recover and rest can be valued rather than seen as a weakness. We *all* need this. So how can we get it?

Building Your Safe Zone

Deciding what kind of space you want will come from what you feel you need in that space. Is it a physical place like your garden, or maybe even a public space like the library? If not, perhaps your safe zone is more a state of mind, where you go when the chaos is caving in on you.

Let's start with the *physical*. If you're looking to find or build a safe space, I'm not asking you to go and get a diploma in bricklaying. Don't overthink it. What you need is to think about what you *want* in that space. I know somebody who *adores* string lights, so in her home she has them in every room. She says they make her feel cozy, and ignite a childlike magic in her mind. Wherever you build your physical safe zone, let it be your sanctuary.

Now for the *emotional*. Safe zones can also be known as *happy places*, and many people have one! I know you didn't ask, but if you really want to know, mine is a small log cabin on the edge of a national park. I just see myself there, looking out onto the never-ending pine trees, and I breathe the fresh air in. If I close my eyes and transport myself there, I feel as though I've immediately got the mind space and calm I need. I feel safer, and I know that's because I've spent a lot of time creating it for myself. Maybe that might work for you, too.

Tools of Kindness

There are tools for strengthening your mind so that you can create any peaceful environment you'd like. To be kind to yourself sometimes means you have to reach out and find an approach that works for you. Believe me when I say that I tried *everything*! These are the three that worked best for me.

Mindfulness. Don't just assume that mindfulness is "living in the moment." It's so much more. It's not just noticing what you're doing; it's being present enough to *feel* it, too. Nothing else exists. The past has gone, the future is not yet written, and all you have is the very second you're in. There are sights, sounds, and smells to captivate you, and they *will* if you allow them. Being mindful on a regular basis will give you the opportunity to separate from your trauma over time, and that time can heal.

Grounding Exercises. Any kind of grounding exercise acts as a way to snap you back into the present moment by connecting to what's around you. Some people like to splash their face with cold water, or let their hands run under the faucet. The cold acts as a distraction from what's going on in your mind—and it *works!* Others like to get outside and place their feet on the ground. It actually creates an electrical connection to the ground, and should be done for at least twenty minutes for good results such as improved mood and sleep.

Affirmations. Tell yourself good things! Honestly, it's the best thing you can instantly do for yourself. It doesn't matter if you don't believe them, because in time you will. *I matter. I am going to have a good day. I love myself. I've got this.*

Whatever works, do that and you will find solace, just like Brie did.

Case Study: Brie

I used to hate walking up any kind of stairs with somebody behind me. I would panic and run, and sometimes I'd trip over, fall and hurt myself. I had no idea why, and it was becoming frustrating to me to not be able to feel safe walking up a single flight of stairs, even when I was in my home.

One day, my parents were over to babysit my son, as I had a work party. It was bathtime, and they clapped their hands and said, "Run up those stairs, or the crocodile will eat you!" My son started to panic and cry and ran as fast as his three-year-old legs could carry him up the stairs.

That was it for me. I knew there and then where my fear came from, and why I panicked even though nothing was ever there. Yes, something so seemingly innocent can have an effect on you as a child, and making sense of it as an adult will give you the freedom from it you need. Now I walk up the stairs slowly and say aloud, "There's nothing behind me; there's nothing behind me." It took time, but it worked!

Practicing Self-Compassion

When it seems as though you're spinning around the drain of life and you can't escape, what do you do to forgive yourself for getting to that point? I used to hate how I treated myself if I made a mistake, or slipped up. If I had a goal I didn't reach, I'd throw the towel in immediately. "*What's the point?!*" I'd yell. "*Why do I even bother?!*"

Eventually, I realized what a cop-out that was. Anger was my excuse. It was what stopped me from escaping that swirling drain. Research shows that having self-compassion actually *lowers* levels of anxiety and depression, meaning you're far more likely to see through those impossible goals you set yourself.

So, what *is* self-compassion? For starters, it is *learnable!* Second, it's the art of showing yourself kindness and forgiveness. It is how you take a deep breath and say, "Well, that didn't go according to plan. But that's *okay.*" Practicing it involves a consistent desire to show yourself that you drive to be treated well. If you do that, it will extend into the world, so that you're treated just as well by people you encounter.

The Magic of Self-Kindness

Who *wants* to be unkind to themselves? I'd say people who are very deeply hurting, and who are ingrained to believe they don't deserve to feel anything near good. Magic *really* unfolds when you start to look at what kindness does to the self.

I say the "self" and not "you" because the self makes you different from everybody else. It is fundamentally and foundationally who you are, and if you're showing it kindness, you're doing good.

Think about it—are you here because you were treated well in the past? Do you have an inner child who needs healing because you had kindness shown and taught to you? Probably not. I'm not here to make you feel terrible, but I *am* here to guide you to an innovative way of treating yourself.

Magic. It's where you start to see opportunities as adventures. It's where you stop thinking that something will go wrong. It's stopping taking the easy way out. It's where you no longer blame yourself when things go wrong. It all starts with being kind to the self, with such actions as:

- *Encouraging yourself, and believing in your abilities.*
- *Making healthier food and drink choices.*
- *Remaining mindful, and knowing that the present is the only time you can alter your path.*
- *Not letting your moods determine your actions.*

Being Proactive When Self-Compassion is Stolen

When self-compassion lacks, or doesn't exist at all, you can still find ways to be proactive. I want to offer one mental exercise and one physical exercise for developing self-compassion in times of pure vulnerability or uncertainty. Both are achievable.

The Awareness. As you grow into self-compassion, being *aware* is key. Notice how you feel. You might be in a situation where you say, "Wow, this feels difficult," or, "Where is the nearest exit? Get me outta here!" Emotions are often noted, but never really *considered*. The whys, the wheres, the familiarity and discomfort rising; it's all there to explore.

Self-Soothing. How do you feel about hugging yourself? No, I haven't gone completely mad! It's a thing! And it is scientifically proven to de-stress and calm the most panicked of people. Other physical ways you can be proactive when you feel like everything is falling apart is by simply placing your hand on your chest and taking a few crucial deep breaths. What you're doing is transforming the way an external factor is making you feel *internally*. That is powerfully transformative.

And speaking of which, let's look at Rose's story.

Case Study: Rose

As a nurse, being kind is part of my job. I spend long hours several times a day caring for people who are sick and need my attention. I always felt the overwhelming desire to help others even as a young girl, and I never put myself first. It's how I got my parents to be pleased with me.

Nursing felt like the natural vocation to follow, but I began to feel drained and tired, and my diet suffered. I ate when I could, and that mostly meant fast food. Eventually, I felt like a different person (and not for the better). Something had to change.

I took some time off work, and got to see some ways in which I'd neglected myself like it was something I'd always experienced. That kindness I was putting out into the world needed to come back to me too, at least in part.

I started to meal-prep on my days off, easy but healthy food. I made sure I listened to a podcast on the way home instead of loud music to relax me. If I had a day off, I'd sleep in and not get up early to binge-watch TV. Little things made all the difference, and I no longer felt so triggered by my job, because that kindness was coming back to me.

Finally.

CHAPTER FOUR

Reconnecting with Your Inner Child

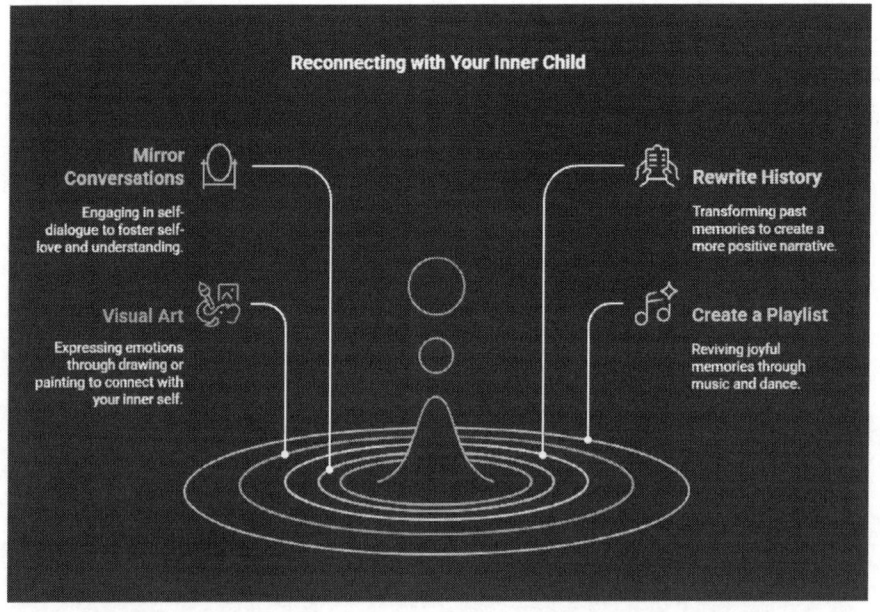

It's never going to be easy reconnecting with your inner child when all you have been taught is to shut them down. That doesn't mean it's impossible, however; in fact, the most empowering move you can make right now is to let them awaken fully, so you can meet them and build a relationship with them.

Meeting Your Inner Child

Meeting your inner child will look and feel different for each person. Here are some accounts from people who have previously done the work, and have their initial thoughts on hand to share:

James, 35: *"I put the first meeting off for longer than I'd care to admit. I dismissed it as nonsense, but at the same time, I felt myself being pulled to give it a go. That first meeting felt like I was finally able to breathe after years of not being able to. It felt like my soul was flowing again."*

Mel, 42: *"I went into meeting my inner child completely unsure of what to expect; but I knew one thing, and that was how gentle I needed to be with myself. It helped to not expect anything, because then I had no preconceptions. I felt instant relief when that moment came. It was as if I was late to an essential appointment, and the moment I felt that connection was when I began to thank her for being there for me, even when I had forgotten her."*

When the time comes, meeting your inner child will feel similar to gazing into a mirror, where that younger, wrinkle-free version of yourself is looking right back at you. You see past the physical, and start to notice all the wounds, emotions, and dreams you learned to bury through your life. It's a moment of sheer tenderness that reawakens vulnerability while simultaneously giving you permission to lean into it. Will you feel slightly crazy at first? Well, here's a secret: *I* did. You might start to notice how joyful, wounded, or hesitant they appear, and that's perfectly normal. There's no right or wrong answer here, and I think that's an essential part to remember.

And for you? If there is laughter, tears, silence or sheer overwhelm, all of it is acceptable as much as it is expectable. Try not to judge yourself—we do far too much of that in life already.

There are two ways you can reach out to your inner child; through *meditation* and by *journaling*. Let's start with the former.

Meditation

Meditation is practiced by over 375 million people all over the world, with 38 million of them *alone* in the US. It is a vital tool in maintaining optimum well-being, but it is much more than just clearing your mind and bringing to life an inner peace we all crave in our hectic lives.

Meditating is known to *relieve stress, depression and anxiety, as well as mild to moderate pain; decrease use of cigarettes, alcohol, and drugs; help spark new creativity; and improve memory.* The best part is that meditation can also be used as a tool for reaching out and connecting with your inner child. A growing numbers of therapists are using it in practice with patients worldwide.

Once upon a time, I know meditating was looked at as something only "hippies" do. Turns out, these people were way ahead of their time, knowing the difference being still can make to your overall well-being. I was completely down for trying, and now I want *you* to do the same.

Guided Meditation

So how do you meditate to meet your inner child? Start in a quiet place that suits you, where you can feel comfortable and, most importantly, safe. It's up to you whether you sit or lay down, whatever works for you.

Close your eyes and start by taking a few deep breaths. This gives your body and mind permission to relax into the moment. Some people like to imagine walking along a warmly lit path, while others like to see themselves somewhere more familiar, like the garden they grew up in or the park near their childhood home. Wherever you want to be, picture yourself there.

As you walk, you come across an inviting space that resonates with you. Once you get to this space, visualize your inner child appearing in front of you. See the smaller version of yourself, and allow their innocence and vulnerabilities to be present. Then, notice how they appear. What are they trying to express? How are they holding themselves? What is their energy? Again, this is going to differ for each person, and there is no right or wrong answer here. Gently approach them with the kindness and awareness for them you're developing. Let them know you're there to listen. You don't have to talk aloud, but you can if you want to.

Now ask your inner child what they need, or if there's anything they'd like to share. It's your moment to offer them the unconditional love they never had, and your reassurance will allow that connection to remain. You may find it helpful to thank them for trusting you, and letting them know that you're there for them. Remind your inner child that they aren't alone; that's so important.

When you're ready, you can open your eyes, knowing that the initial meeting has occurred. Any subsequent meetings will begin to feel more real and more available to you now.

Journaling

Famous psychologist *James Pennebaker* conducted research into journaling and found it is positively impactful toward our nervous system, so that's why I couldn't leave it out. Lacking conscious awareness of our inner child can lead to feelings of dis-ease in the mind and body, so anything that can level out the nervous system *will* help you heal. I've developed five ways to help you get started in your journaling journey. Pick out the most suitable approach for *you*.

Childhood Memory Reflection. Think of a vivid memory from your childhood, and how it made you feel in that moment. Now, think about how those feelings influence you today in all aspects of life and what you do.

Identify a Core Belief. Back when you were a child, you heard messages about yourself and the world around you. Think about whether those messages limited you or empowered you. How do they show up now?

Go Back to Moments That Feel Painful. I know it may sound counterproductive, but recalling a time you felt hurt, or maybe scared or misunderstood as a child, can help you think about what you needed in that moment that you didn't receive.

Explore Your Past Playfulness. Thinking back to your childhood, what brought you joy, even if you weren't able to express it fully? Think of either experiences or activities, and think about how you can start to introduce them to your adult self.

Write a Letter to Your Inner Child. Think about what you'd like to say or share with your younger self, and write down whatever reassurance or acknowledgement they need. Remember, you're there to offer love and support.

Whatever way you choose to connect with your inner child, please know that it is going to be the first time in a long time you've felt seen and heard. *Ruth* can vouch for this in her account below.

Case Study: Ruth

I don't think you can prepare for meeting your inner child for the first time, because you simply don't know what to expect. Even if you have an idea, it's never going to feel that exact way.

For me, growing up in a strict household meant that something as innocent as playing and having fun felt more like a luxury I was never allowed rather than the right of any child. My parents both valued work and discipline above everything else, and any moment spent on "being pathetic" always earned me a sharp reprimand. I carried that all the way into adulthood. It felt natural, but not nice, to chase achievement while feeling hollow inside.

One evening, I just broke down. I had concerned myself with the concept of guided meditation before, reading about it but not having the courage to approach it fully. But I had to try something! I closed my eyes and gave myself a moment to focus on my breath. I felt spiritually encouraged to imagine a safe, warm place, so I pictured a meadow in the spring, glowing in sunlight. It was beautiful and calm, two things my soul was lacking at the time.

Slowly, a little girl emerged. She was a version of me at around six years old. She even had messy hair and that nervous twitch I had, where I curled up my clothes in my fingers. An initial awkwardness arose, and I felt almost silly, but I had to try to spark my curiosity further. I'd had enough of ignoring what I knew I had to do. "What do you want to tell me?" I whispered (out loud!).

Her response wasn't words, just a look that made my chest ache with sadness. I remembered it well. She needed my help, and I was the only one who could give it.

When the meditation came to a natural end, I picked up a notebook and, using my non-dominant hand, let my inner child speak. It felt like the right thing to do.

The writing was clumsy, but her words came thick and fast.

"I'm lonely. I want to play. Do you see me?"

I hadn't played in years.

That moment was when everything changed for me. I promised younger me that I'd listen and start making time and space for more joy, however small that may be.

It took a few weeks, but I started bringing activities to life just for fun. I painted, I danced, and I even took my niece to the park to blow bubbles!

Meeting my inner child involved being vulnerable, and that felt strange, but it also felt like coming home to a part of myself I'd forgotten was there. I had a lot of making up to do.

Listening To What Your Inner Child Needs

How often have you had that emotional pull in your gut telling you to lean into an unfamiliar or intimidating emotion? You want to run, but you *need* to stick around. This is what *listening to your inner child* looks and feels like, and it's another way to grow and heal.

Be curious. Blocking out what we know we need to face doesn't make it go away. Like with any trauma, it'll still be there, and will make itself known further along your path, often in a much more alarming way next time. Meeting those needs can improve your chances of healing.

Unmet Needs and Their Impact On Living Mindfully

Let's look more at your own unmet needs, and how they are preventing you from living in the present moment. What do *you* think I mean by "unmet needs?" This isn't about not having any pizza in the fridge! When asked, the most common response are answers like, "I don't give myself enough time to relax," or, "People just don't listen to or understand me."

But guess what? It always goes *a lot* deeper than that. If you have unmet needs, you can bet your bottom dollar that they can be traced back to childhood. At times, your voice was never heard, no matter how loudly you spoke. Your feelings were never paid attention to, so you were never validated. Nobody had your back.

These are *basic needs,* and when neglected can disengage a person from their inner child and hinder the way they live and thrive into adulthood. Suddenly, patterns of anxiety and self-doubt can become the new norm, as well as one of the worst side effects of needs not being met: *Avoidance.* As you avoid what you need to do, you learn quickly that the moment you're in is not the moment you are mentally living.

There *is* a solution to that, and it's where I want you to begin basing all thoughts and actions from now on. The answer is to be as intentional with living mindfully as you have been with avoiding your pain.

You Owe Yourself Empathy and Understanding

Learning to respond to your inner child with empathy and understanding is vital if you want to notice change, and in doing so will activate the brain's *mirror neurons*. This mirror can act as the same one you see your inner child in, and will help you empathize with what they (you) went through.

To understand empathy is to offer yourself that understanding directly. It is how you learn to forgive yourself for a past you couldn't control as a child in the way you can now. This is about teaching yourself to be open to receiving something long overdue, and connecting more deeply to yourself emotionally.

If we're going to get into the science of it all, I want to do so by thinking about the positive aspects of responding with empathy to your inner child. As you do, your brain releases oxytocin, which is known as the *bonding hormone*, which reinforces how safe you feel, and how connected you feel to your inner child. Neuroscience proves that when you start to display compassion, you can rewire old patterns of fear and neglect that have been stored in the amygdala all this time. What an amazing process! You'll be feeling more confident in no time.

Inner Child Communication Exercises

So how exactly do you communicate with your inner child? I've got five exercises that will give you a huge connection boost.

Mirror Conversations. Look into a mirror and speak to your inner child. It's that simple. Phrases such as *"I see you and I love you"* will build a connection, and help you understand that it's never too late to love. Don't be afraid!

Rewrite History. Rewriting a childhood story or memory to make the ending more comforting, reassuring, or positive will help reframe painful memories. Give yourself what you need.

Visual Art. Draw or even paint a picture that represents your inner child's emotions. Use that as the basis for responding to it with another as your adult self.

Create a Playlist. Creating a playlist of songs you loved to dance or sing along as a child will open up a level of freedom within you that was previously locked away by your unchosen limitations.

Engage With Childhood Stuffed Animals. Sometimes, people like to see or hold something tangible in order to help them. If you have a stuffed animal from childhood that resonates with you, you can hold it and talk to it as if it's your inner child. If you don't have a stuffed animal left over from childhood, you can always buy a new one from the store and talk to it. If it makes you feel better, you can tell the store clerk it's a birthday gift for your niece (I won't tell).

Building a Relationship with Your Inner Child

Building a relationship with your inner child is a profound journey of self-discovery. Carl Jung once said, *"The most terrifying thing is to accept oneself completely."* It's perfectly true, and often what prevents people from truly taking on any healing challenge. What's left after the hardest parts of healing are fragments of a person you don't even know, and it can be scary to some.

"What if I don't like that person? What if I don't know how to 'be' them?" These "what ifs" come from the part of your brain that just wants to protect you, but this is the same part that doesn't know right from wrong. This leaves you with trust, which will carry you forward and connect you, your adult self, to your inner child. My Three Pillars of Connection are designed to help you form a connection between two people who are overdue to meet!

Pillar Number 1: Write With Your Non-Dominant Hand. Writing with your non-dominant hand is encouraged by art therapists all over the world, and is great for saying hi to your inner child. It involves slowing down and allowing thoughts to come to your mind that flow to paper through what appears to be childlike writing. When you visually see that writing, it will prompt you to feel and remember that child you once were, and allow your inner child's voice to come to the surface. Write letters, thoughts, whatever makes you feel comfortable. This is one occasion where it's okay for your writing to be terrible!

Pillar Number 2: Affirmations. Affirmations are positive, short phrases you can use to help you both build trust with yourself and give your inner child time to move positively toward you in a safe space. *I hear you. You're safe with me. You matter. You're not alone.* These aren't just words; they can become the foundation and basis of everything you believe about yourself and the young child who had a very hard time.

Pillar Number 3: Play Time...Again! It's never too late to play! What did you love as a child? Were you a budding performer? Did you love to bake? What can you do in tribute to your inner child to let them know you're still there, and you're committed to them?

Maintaining a Daily Connection

Small moments of conscious work add up to the most worthwhile results when it comes to maintaining daily connections. These are the three main ways you can do that in your life:

Check In on the AM. Check in with your inner child every morning. Ask them how they feel, or what they need today. Don't judge what comes back at you; what you offer yourself is a new level of self-awareness that wasn't there before.

Create Moments for Creativity. If creativity is your thing, sometimes you just need a moment. I mean, there's nothing quite like doodling when you're on hold to your boss, or maybe playing some kind of word puzzle that you always enjoyed as a child.

Make Compassion a Habit. You're going to be met with challenges, but that's the time you need to be the kindest to yourself. How would you speak to a friend or an upset child? I would bet a lot of money it'd be different to how you might usually talk to yourself if in the same situation. Acknowledge a difficult day by wrapping yourself up in a blanket and telling yourself that you tried your best.

When you learn to drive, you don't just get in a car and know it all. It takes practice. Time. Patience. Knowledge. It's the same with anything else you practice, and connecting daily is the way to do that. After all, this is what establishes *trust* between your adult self, and your inner child, as Robert below will explain.

Case Study: Robert

I can tell you one thing for sure—I never thought I'd sit at home in the evening talking to my inner child. Two years ago, that idea would have had me laughing until my stomach hurt. Luckily my neighbors haven't knocked out of concern for my welfare…yet.

It's now a regular thing for me, and that's due to not giving up on it. At times I wanted to, believe me. It took a good while for my younger self to even trust me. He saw I had turned up, and I could tell he was angry. For a few months, I thought it was aimed at me, but I learned that this anger was hiding a world of sadness and neglect. He'd felt abandoned, and he had every right. But it wasn't my fault, and it was such a relief to discover.

My therapist called it "inner child trust." It was a process, not just a moment or event that would make everything better. It was messy at times, but that mess was made so that I could clear it away and find nuggets of truth in the mental clutter.

I lost track of the number of times I saw my inner child cross his arms at me, as if it were a defense. I lived with that defense for decades, and I had to go back and fix it to free my present self. I made promises, and then I kept them. Eventually, young me went from anger to intrigue. He wanted to go on the walks I told him we'd do. I picked up my guitar more, and I learned songs I liked as a kid.

I suffered the odd setback if work was really busy, or if I was unwell. I'd always reach out and let my inner child know that I'd be back as soon as I could, and it felt like those moments bridged otherwise destructive gaps. I learned that the best things, like self-discovery, can feel like breaking down the strongest barriers, but that's precisely what makes them mean something.

Chapter Five

Reparenting Yourself

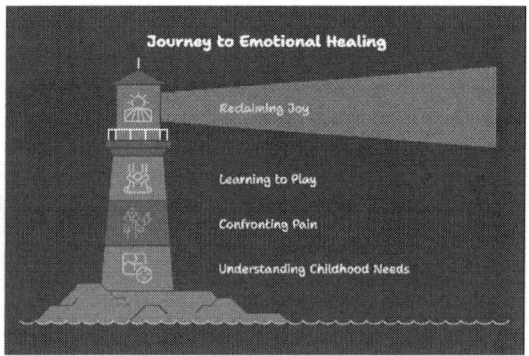

If our childhoods were where we learned what relationships looked like and meant, and how to process how we feel, then that also means it's where we learned about boundaries, and every other habit and behavior. We watched others, we absorbed our environment, and we figured out a way to survive. Where does *reparenting* fit into this?

Ideally, you would have had loving parents who had a high level of self-awareness and unending love for you—but we don't live in that kind of world. If your parents *came* from a wounded place, then that wounded place is where they will likely continue to operate from. Parents can only love and *be* that parent from the level of awareness they know.

So, what does that mean for you? If you had that love, the chances are the way you talk to yourself is kind and confident. Your needs were tended to, so you learned how to tend to them yourself as you got older. If you didn't receive that love, you'll know that feeling of something being missing—something *big*. It's hard to put your finger on an emptiness so big, and it's difficult to miss what you never really had.

Reparenting yourself is how you give *back* to yourself what you didn't receive as a child. The concept is proven to heal those childhood wounds you've been carrying around with you, so you can function more efficiently and fill those holes from your past with love and emotional nourishment.

Reparenting can look like:

- Reclaiming joy
- Learning how to play
- Confronting your pain
- Looking at what you didn't receive as a child

The benefits of reparenting will offer you insight and practice in how to validate your emotions. No longer will you ignore what's going on inside; you'll be able to address and work with them. Because every child deserves unconditional love and support, these can be things you can provide for yourself. In time, you will begin to feel safe and secure (think back to emotional safety), and that will provide a new level of consistency for you. A stable life is what we should all have.

What a transformative journey you will embark on the moment you consciously decide to reparent yourself. There's nothing more empowering than realizing you can provide yourself with what you need (overdue, I'm sure you'll agree). I've got eight tips for you to ignite your mind into the concept of reparenting, and how you can get started.

Affirm Your Decision to Reparent. What brought you here? What was that *"eureka"* moment? Now use that to affirm your choice to do so. *I am a good person. I am worth it.*

Talk to Yourself. This doesn't have to be *literal*, but talking to yourself means you can connect with what you need from an outside perspective. Help yourself make daily decisions that encourage reparenting.

Reward Yourself Every Day. In healthy ways, seek to reinforce your journey and reward yourself every day. A thank you, a long bath, hugging yourself, whatever you need that is good.

Get the Zzzs In. Sleep is essential, and *good* sleep awakens your well-being and emotional balance.

Use a Notebook. Any achievements can be quickly forgotten if you're struggling with a positive outlook, so notebooks are a great way to record them. You're trying to celebrate your progress!

Continue Your Mindfulness Practices. By now, you know how mindfulness will keep you in the present moment, so any ways you've learned tools for mindfulness can help here.

Self-love All the Way. Might it be uncomfortable? Yes. Might it even be drastically unfamiliar to you? Of course. Does that mean you can't love yourself and push through? No!

Reflect on the Existing Good and Create New Good. Reflecting on any good memories from your childhood will help you, especially if you add in making brand-new positive memories you have the power and ability to make today.

Daily Practices to Reparent

Affirmations

What is more reinforcing than positive self-talk? Affirmations can get forgotten, because you must consciously decide to say something good to yourself when you aren't used to doing so. It can feel uncomfortable, and you may not even believe it at first.

It was Mel Robbins who invented the "high-five to yourself," and she was really onto something. It can seem like a lot to initially offer yourself, though, and that's where words come in. *I did great today. I am learning how to be there for myself. I am on a journey, and I am valuing each day.*

Start small by accepting that the steps to healing are there to take one at a time.

Self-talk Scripts

Scripts are written every day. Why should it be any different for you? You deserve to write a script for yourself to read and remember every day. Practicing it will allow you to become that person you're writing about. It might sound like the following:

I will remember to give myself this opportunity to heal today. At work I will take things one step at a time, and handle problems the best way I can. When I get home, I will catch up with a few friends and make a delicious dinner to share with my family. After that and before bed, I am going to set aside an hour for myself, to relax and take care of myself—a bath, a glass of wine, and some reading by candlelight.

Nurturing Routines

If you want to raise resilient kids, you need to create nurturing routines, and the same thing is true for your inner child. Nurturing routines act like warm blankets; the trick is to understand what feels good, and repeat it where possible. Think about why you're doing what you're doing, and encourage positive self-talk when you do it.

For example, if you're trying to apply insulation tape to your doors and windows to keep warm in the winter, start with one window and take your time. Make sure the tape is straight, and then close it to feel the difference. As you're applying the tape, tell yourself what a great job you're doing, and how much you're tending to your needs. Soon, your whole house will be warmer with less draft. *You* did that. You took the initiative to want to be warmer.

Let's look at how Hannah found safety in how she reparented herself.

Case Study: Hannah

On the outside, I had everything; two parents, a nice house. I went to a good school, and everything I wanted or needed, my parents got for me. To everybody else, it looked like there was nothing to complain about.

Except, I never saw them. Dad was the CEO of a huge company, and my mom was always out with her friends, going on vacation and, I quote, "enjoying her life." I had to fend for myself a lot, and on bad days where I'd have a hard pop quiz in school, I'd come home and have nobody to talk to. If I needed support, money was thrown at me and I'd get a tutor or a babysitter.

I had this house that screamed "comfort," yet I felt nowhere near safe in it. I'd be told to order takeout for dinner as my parents were always busy or out. Money didn't matter, but evidently, neither did I.

When I got older, I knew I didn't want to be with somebody who made lots of money but at the expense of putting work first. As long as we could live, pay the bills and enjoy a yearly vacation, I was happy. I found that man, and now we have a daughter. She's our world. We were both there for her first steps, her school recitals, and all her hockey games.

I learned fast that in order to give another human what I never had, I had to offer the same level of compassion to myself. I had had to take care of my needs from a young age; but as I grew up, I realized I needed those needs to be more emotional, rather than essential.

I did that by seeing my childhood as a pattern of holes that needed to be filled. I discovered what brought me joy, and I added it to my home. Plants, three cats, three dogs (and a lizard my daughter insisted on!), lots of color, and home cooking.

I like to keep a mood diary for myself, and I have three different colored pens to write with (red, orange and green). They act like traffic lights; so if I had a hard day, I'll write in red, etc. It's my way of logging how I'm feeling, and what I found hard that particular day, but it's great to reflect on at the end of each week.

I started small, but I got to know myself and what a home should feel and be like. And now not only does my daughter get to have that, but I do, too. I finally feel safe.

Emotional Regulation Techniques

Learning to regulate your emotions works wonders in calming your nervous system, which was probably left with sensitive reactions due to any trauma you experienced. You can find ideal tools to help you regulate, especially when you feel distressed. This part of healing is crucial, so I want you to get comfy and really dig in.

Checking In With Your Nervous System

The nervous system is like the control center for your whole body and mind. The autonomic part of your nervous system is responsible for your emotional well-being, and that can be broken down into two main parts: *the sympathetic* and *the parasympathetic.*

The sympathetic is where you'll find your "fight-or-flight" response. If there's a threat, *that* part will awaken *quickly*—sweaty palms, racing heart—preparing you for "battle." The parasympathetic part of your nervous system activates when it's time to recover, helping you to find calm.

The problem is when the battle in question is a trauma, a memory, or a trigger. Those symptoms of panic still arise because the nervous system knows no better. It's *a lot*. Stress can leave your panic button switched on with just a thought, and as it constantly wants to protect you, it brings you little peace.

Here are some tools for helping you find the switch for your parasympathetic system. and *finding* that inner peace:

Move Your Body. Moving in any way will relieve stress; you don't have to be an athlete to do so! Exercise, move, let your body flow, and the tension will immediately begin to leave your body and feel more relaxed.

Weighted Blanket. I'll get personal here, because I sleep with a weighted blanket *most nights*. I love them; the pressure helps me feel as though the universe has my back. Every night, I just melt into my mattress.

Meditate. There's *nothing* meditation can't help you with, I can promise you. Focus on a breath or a phrase to get you to your happy place.

Sing or Laugh. Fun fact! The main nerve in your parasympathetic system is called the *vagus nerve*. It's proven to relax if you sing or laugh, because the vagus nerve is stimulated when doing so.

Tapping. The Emotional Freedom Technique (EFT) has emerged to be a *fantastically effective* practice to help you achieve a sense of calm. Areas common for tapping with your fingers are your outer palm, the middle of your forehead, below your nose and lip, and your chest to name a few. It's well worth looking into, and is even used in therapy sessions all over the world. Studies have shown that there is a decrease in symptoms in those who suffer with PTSD of over 23 percent after an EFT intervention. Moreso, a study of 5000 patients who sought treatment for anxiety saw a *90 percent* improvement after tapping, compared to 63 percent of those who only tried Cognitive Behavioral Therapy (CBT).

EFT is just one approach to helping you regulate your parasympathetic system, but the evidence proves its effectiveness in many.

Bringing in The Breath and Senses

Deeper strategies involving breathing and the five senses can really help you dig deep when you need to, and there's always something suitable for everybody. Two strategies known to widely work include:

Lion's Breath. Popular in yoga. Spread your fingers apart and take a deep breath in through your nose. Stick out your tongue and stretch it down to your chin.

Let out a large breath, forcing the air across your tongue. Make a "ha" sound deep down from your abdomen. Have a little moment to break by breathing normally, and then begin once more.

Abdomen Breathing. Research shows that abdominal (or diaphragmatic breathing) reduces mental and physical stress. Put one hand on your chest and one just below your ribcage. Breathe slowly in through your nose, being aware of the air moving down to your abdomen. In doing this, your stomach will expand outwards, but your chest should remain stable and still. Purse your lips, exhaling slowly for three seconds. Think about how your stomach expands and contracts, but your chest makes only slight movements. This is how you can steadily breathe to reignite relaxation.

Progressive Muscle Relaxation. Progressive muscle relaxation (PMR) is the process of consciously noticing the tension in your body, while actively proving that you can relax it. It's almost like a memory you're creating, so that your body learns to relax more easily. Here are specific parts of your body you can use in PMR:

- *Fists* - Clench both fists, holding then letting go
- *Biceps* - Bend your elbows, tense muscles before relaxing
- *Forehead* - Wrinkle your forehead into a frown and hold before releasing
- *Eyes* - Close your eyes tight, and hold before letting go
- *Jaw* - Gently clench your jaw before releasing
- *Tongue* - Press it up into the roof of your mouth and hold, then release
- *Neck* - Press your neck back gently and hold, before letting go and slowly leaning forward to stretch
- *Shoulders* - Shrug your shoulders as high as you're comfortably able to while holding stomach out, then hold before letting go
- *Lower Back* - Gently arch up and release again

Visualization

If you're an elite athlete, you're most likely already *using visualization techniques*. This is about mind over matter; picturing what you want, then aiming for it.

Imagining outcomes will help carry you toward them in real time; so if that outcome is to reparent yourself, then visualization may be just for you!

Picture and Describe. The more detail you imagine where you want to be, the more real it will come alive in your mind. Specific mental images create room in your brain for it to manifest and build, and that's how we stay rooted to our goals.

Use Index Cards. Remember flashcards from school? There's nothing stopping you from using them as an adult. Write down what you want in detail, one on each card, then look through them before bed each night.

Vision Board. You can have a digital version on your phone or computer, or you can make a *physical* version in your home. Pictures, memes, quotes—whatever you want. This is *your* time to build what inspires you to keep going, something you can look at every day.

CHAPTER SIX

Cultivating Self-Love

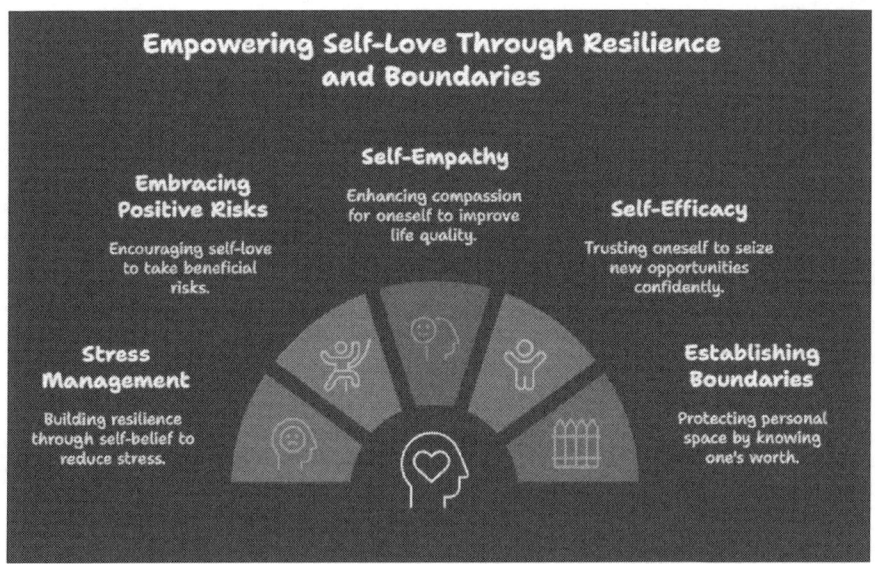

Self-love is a lucrative industry now, said to be just under half a trillion dollars. You can see it in all the blogs, magazines, and TV shows, and hear it in the voices of friends, strangers, and podcasts: *Look after yourself, and everything else will be*

fine! Overwhelming, isn't it? I for one got lost in the concept for a while, assuming all I needed was a bath and a haircut.

Self-love is *so much more*. If you lacked love as a child, you will feel even more polarizing thoughts about it. *How can I learn to love myself? Is there enough time for me to get all the self-love I need to make up for the time I went without? What if I feel guilty for paying attention to myself for once? What does it even look like to cultivate self-love?*

I want you to erase all preconceptions now. *Building* self-love is not the same as *expressing* it. It's not as easy as simply loving yourself first before anybody else truly can. If you were deprived of love as a child, how can you muster the strength to flip that switch to on, and show yourself in an instant that you matter?

Self-love is a skill. It's one you can learn to be the master of, if you give yourself the opportunity. In order to do that, you just need to understand it in more detail.

Understanding Self-Love

You're building up an idea of self-love in your mind, but you stop short at being able to execute it for yourself. It seems crazy to think that you can love yourself into life again when nobody is really guiding you, but self-love is about trusting yourself enough to be the guide.

This is *not* what turns people into narcissists. Self-love is to view your strengths as equally as you do your weaknesses—you as a whole—and accept it all. You need to learn how to love yourself properly if you're going to take chances, build a new life for yourself, see the world differently, and hold yourself accountable for your goals and dreams.

Here are *five benefits of self-love* that you can take away with you today:

Stress Less. Stress comes from the feeling of being incapable. It's well within your power to build your resilience and see that you can lower it by believing in yourself and handling any challenges head on.

Risks—The Good Kind! Do you want to go for it? What's stopping you! And there you go, listing all the reasons why you *shouldn't*, when a little self-love will prove that you should, and can!

Empathy: The Real Winner. Have compassion for yourself, and see the real winner. If having a life coach can improve your empathy by over 40 percent, imagine what being your *own* life coach can do for you.

Self-Efficacy. What do you think it means to trust yourself? If you love yourself in a way that encourages you to take on new opportunities and believe you can execute them, you will feel less overwhelmed.

Boundaries. Why offer a dishonest *yes* when you can provide an honest *no*? Ultimately, boundaries are there to protect you and whatever it is you do or don't want to do. You have that choice now, and building them only comes from truly knowing your worth, and *not* listening to the myths!

Self-Love Myths

Self-love doesn't mean being selfish or greedy, only thinking your opinion counts, or blaming/shaming. Let's look closer at each of these.

Selfishness. Let's make no mistake—selfishness comes from believing you're perfect, and that it's everybody else's job to fix you. It's not. And no amount of self-love will grow from that.

Only Thinking Your Opinion Counts. Opinions are shared, and should be valued in this world. We don't always all agree, but we should listen. If you can listen to how others love themselves, you can widely find success stories.

Greed. Don't think that being greedy with your time and who you give it to will equate to higher levels of self-love; it won't. With greed comes the opposite of self-love; in fact, it will turn you into somebody you don't particularly like.

The Shame/Blame Barriers. We all hit barriers, but if we know what they are, we can prepare for their appearance. Two of the most powerful are shame and blame.

Brené Brown likens shame to a silent epidemic that encourages negative behavior and thoughts. She believes shame leads to feelings of unworthiness, and the belief that you are somehow flawed. I wonder if you might currently agree, as you navigate what it means to fully embrace self-love. If we were to all think like Brené, we would understand that to truly connect with ourselves, we need to accept that "*not being enough*" is a belief that only sets us to spiral downward, and not upward.

Shame leads to rejecting yourself, and that's the opposite of what you should be doing right now. Think about it. When you were a child, you believed everything your parents told you. *The sun is so hot! That dog might bite, be careful. It's late, you need to go to bed. It's time for school, the bus is on its way.* That makes it tempting to believe everything they said: *You were a mistake! I wish I never had kids.* It is these phrases where you find your shame is born.

Blame is where you sit when you can not move forward, and it cannot exist in the same timeframe as self-love. It acts as a way to cope and self-regulate. *I didn't go for that job because I knew I wouldn't get it. I should have studied harder in school.* What's really going on with that phrase when broken down is the inability to believe you can achieve something good for yourself, and blaming your study habits in school for that. This shouldn't act as a reassurance for you, and I want you to start understanding that your inner critic can prove to be powerful.

These myths will challenge you, but you are bigger than your challenges, and you are bigger than any shame or blame barrier, too.

Combat Your Inner Critic

It's time to combat your inner critic! The voice that insists on being negative *will* keep holding you back unless you learn where it comes from, and how to quiet it, with these five ways.

- You have to stop denying the voice. It's there, it's loud a lot of the time, and ignoring it won't make it go away.

- There's no point in arguing with it. All that will do is build inner conflict—and it's you who will suffer.

- If your inner critic is trying to keep you small, why keep listening to it? Expanding your comfort zone is the only way to destroy what has so far controlled you.

- Think about the long term. In time, that inner voice will become smaller and smaller as you begin to build new habits, and more importantly a new dialogue.

- Your inner critic is a mixture of your low confidence and all previous voices who may have wanted to keep you small. Now you get to create a new inner voice.

Building Self-Worth

Ironically, your inner critic is trying to keep you safe. All the shame that comes with trying something and failing will raise that voice to a point so loud, you can hear nothing else. It's down to you to become determined to prove it wrong. Much of that needs to come from building your self-worth.

Building self-worth is like building yourself a house of kindness, only this is the type of kindness you only give to yourself. I know it can seem daunting, like anything new, when you are looking to hugely change a part of you that's been written already. Nothing is non-erasable, though.

Let's learn to silence the inner critic and find your positivity.

Ssh! Let's Get Positive!

Stop telling me what I can't do, and start telling me what I can *do*! This is the kind of talk you need to have with yourself every day (minus any anger), and start your journey.

Name It!

"Oh here we go, Debbie Downer is in town!" Almost belittle it, like it means nothing to you. Eventually, it *will* mean nothing.

Challenge anything negative that arises.

"Really? Is that a fact, or am I just thinking myself into failure again? What evidence do I have?" Thoughts *are not facts*. You need to understand this completely. It is down to yourself-worth to figure out how to silence your inner critic, and as you will learn, they all go hand in hand.

Reinforcement Exercises For Self-Worth and Confidence

There's no stronger way to believe that you are capable than building on new thoughts and habits. Try these three things when you need to.

Change the script. Go from "I can't" to "I'm going to give it my all!" Your negative narrative is outdated, and is no longer serving you.

Fake it 'til you make it. I know this seems like you're lying to yourself, but in fact, you're working on convincing yourself of a story that you soon won't need to fake. Believe you can, and you will. People do it all the time; now it's your turn!

Ignore social media for a little while. Platforms for comparison are all over the internet, and we're all joined to at least one. Time to step back and work on yourself until you feel ready.

Self-doubt comes from a series of beliefs that have kept you safe from *everything*, *both* good and bad. It's time to let the light in, just like Lucy did.

Case Study: Lucy

I didn't know that how I had been feeling all these years had led to self-doubt. What I mean by that is, I was just so unaware. I just thought it was who I was fundamentally.

I doubted my abilities all through my training to be a nurse, but wanting to be a nurse was something I've always wanted. That wasn't easy for me, but this vocation was in my heart, and all I knew.

In the end, I had to go with what I could see on paper. It was the only way I knew I was worthy of working in the healthcare field. I passed all my exams with flying colors, and my work placements were really successful.

Despite growing up in a home where there was a lot of pressure on me to succeed but very little encouragement to do so, I got to where I wanted to be because my tutors became my inspiration. They gave me the opportunity to become the person I am today, and any self-doubt I had was quickly counteracted by the facts. I think that's what people need to start doing. Stop listening to your thoughts; question them instead, because they are not facts.

Practicing Gratitude and Joy

Practicing anything you're not familiar with can be a great mental goal. When you first start working toward it in those initial few days, you're going to want to run from it. *What do you mean, I can be grateful? What does it even mean to be grateful in this life? I don't even know what joy is, let alone actively live through it!*

You're wrong. You *can* live through a joyous experience. You can live through it by *allowing* it. You deserve it. Nobody taught you that, and that's left you feeling uneasy about even attempting to combat the concept, but that shouldn't stop you now. Look how far you've come, and what you've already achieved.

Gratitude's Gravitational Pull Toward Healing and Self-Acceptance

Gratitude and joy are no different; they're equally as magnetic, as you're about to discover. When you start living a life with gratitude, you need to give it enough time to make it a habit before you begin to associate it with healing. Initially, it can just be nice. It's nice to see the sun rise on a day off, or to enjoy your favorite movie snuggled under a blanket.

If I could give you any snap lesson in what gratitude is, it'd look like this: When you are thirsty, and you head to the kitchen for a glass of water, gratitude is watching the water pour into that glass while thinking about its journey there.

It's such an automatic thing, isn't it? You need a drink, you get one. But in a world where multiple millions of people don't have access to clean water, it's a legitimate thing to be grateful for. Even if you had nothing but bad experiences as a child, you can separate clean water from that abuse. Start *that* simple, and you will find that gratitude has a healthily addictive gravitational pull that you can neither avoid nor resist.

Where does that leave you when it comes to accepting yourself? Self-acceptance and gratitude work well together. Gratitude helps you understand the limits you imposed on yourself, and proves that you can lift the lid of recognizing your own abilities. What you once thought was impossible, in finding or looking for joy in a world that has previously wronged you, is now possible.

Look For Joy and You Will Find It

Who will admit that they consciously look for joy? Can I get a show of hands? Looking for joy isn't like watching Will Ferrell in *Elf* jump across New York crossings and peel gum off the sidewalk. I don't want you to think you need to force yourself so much that you lose yourself completely the other way.

Rediscovering joy can be gentle. It can be in the small, intrinsic moments of life that you once bypassed on your way to worry or fear. Joy doesn't need to be added up throughout your day on a calculator. There's no mark to meet; there's just *intent*. If you intend to look for it, it will find you.

I say this because if you look for fear or worry, that will always find you, too. Well, I say, if you can look for the negative, why not look for the positive? Gratitude is seeing the good in a world where there is always bad around, and I understand the challenge in this when you're either having a bad day, or you're wired to feel unable to do so.

Start by thinking about what brings you joy in your life. Take one thing, even if it's seeing the blue sky, or hearing the soft rain against your window as you get into bed at night. Start to get to know this feeling. Think about what you get from seeing or hearing what you love. Extend that wider into your day, and look for whenever else you feel that same sense of purpose. Are you grateful for the "good morning" from your neighbor when you cross paths? Do you love it when you set your alarm five minutes early so you have time for a drive-thru coffee on the way to work?

What do you consciously practice each day that opens the door wide for subconscious joy that you can bring to the surface of your awareness? Let *those* be the things you're grateful for, and allow them to be the foundation for all other joy, just like Ben did.

Case Study: Ben

I made the mistake of thinking that healing from my childhood meant I had to do one big thing. I know that sounds crazy, but I didn't think healing could mean a million different ways to feel better.

Healing had always been explained to me like I had to wake up and "do it." I thought, "How?!" I started to think about all the ways life brings joy my way, and how I block it all. Every opportunity for happiness or growth was a no-no. I hated it, but at the same time I wanted it so badly.

Feeling happy was a new concept for me, but it was especially new because I didn't know how to create situations that made me happy. I felt it was all too much to try and do, and that's where I kept falling down.

My life started to turn around the day my favorite band released a new album. I put it on to listen to from start to finish, and it was like a journey of nostalgia—but a positive one! It felt so good hearing them again, and it made me feel really happy. From there, I picked up my guitar for the first time in over a decade. I strummed a little, then started learning some of their new songs. The more I played, the happier I felt.

I suddenly realized that as a child, I was repeatedly told not to make too much noise, even though my parents bought me a guitar. Weird, isn't it?! Now I was an adult, I could play as much as I wanted to, and I felt like my soul, which now thinking about it I realize is my inner child, thanked me for it.

These moments may have been small to some, but to me they were actually fairly huge. That album acted as the catalyst for my healing, and at the grand age of 44, I started a band! We meet weekly and just jam, hang out, and play music in my garage. There's no age limit on rock and roll!

CHAPTER SEVEN

Establishing Healthy Boundaries

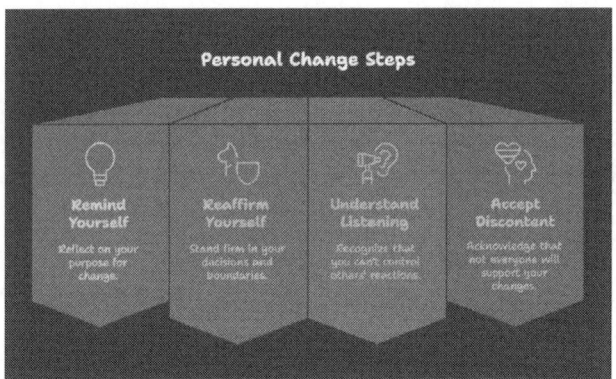

Gathering up all that you need to heal—learning to say no, avoiding people or situations that drain your energy, putting your self-care first, and making sure you have a great support system—all involve establishing healthy boundaries. It's not easy when you don't know where to start, but luckily we can work through it all together. Your boundaries will come alive when you start to understand why you've struggled with them.

Recognizing Boundary Issues

When life feels as though it's pulling you in a dozen different directions, you can usually find your difficulty with boundaries at the center of it all. Seeing as they derive from your core beliefs, opinions, and values, if you don't know what those are, your boundaries will run loose, like sheep breaking free from a farm because the fence fell down.

I have five ways you can immediately tell if you have boundary issues:

Decision Making is a Challenge. If you forever do what others want you to do, how do you know what it is *you* want or need? Decisions can scare or intimidate you, and because of that, you have no idea where to even begin.

You Defer Your Own Wishes Over Fear of Letting People Down. Go along with the plans of others, and you will forever abandon your own. Your desire to not let people down is always going to see you letting yourself down.

You Fear Being Rejected. Your inability to form strong boundaries can be chased all the way back to your childhood. In order to avoid being abandoned, you did what other people told you to do.

You're Constantly Exhausted. I wouldn't be surprised if you were exhausted. Ignoring boundaries is a learned behavior, and often the caregivers we were raised by didn't care about their *own* boundaries.

Your Relationships Are Difficult. Starting from a young age, you will have found out that relationships are tough for you. If you are signaling to others that you cannot make good choices or build strong boundaries, you're more likely to be taken full advantage of.

Your Childhood vs. Your Boundaries

While it may not be the first thing you do, linking your boundary difficulties with your childhood has been extensively studied to the point where clinicians have outlined four patterns common to experiences with boundaries. You may be familiar with them, but have you connected them with boundaries before?

Fight. When needs are thrust onto others, a person can almost attack them to preserve themselves. This may have looked like a parent in your childhood.

Flight. If you haven't got anybody you feel close to, anxiety can increase and you can avoid expressing what you need to them at times. This is how people can be drawn to self-isolation as adults.

Freeze. Zoning out, procrastination; that general feeling of, "If I forget about it, it will go away." It never does.

Fawn. Being emotionally needy to the point where you will do anything for a person who shows you the tiniest breadcrumb of love or attention.

Sometimes, this desire to please in childhood can spill into your adult self, too, as Mark learned.

Case Study: Mark

I was growing sick and tired of my boss calling me whenever work wasn't in session. I applied for and got the job I had because it was something I really wanted. It was the type where you could walk in at nine, walk out at five, and leave everything there once you went home. I wanted that for myself, after seeing my parents and their levels of stress as a kid. That wouldn't be me! Except...it started to be me when I would get texts or calls at 10:00 at night. I wasn't on call, I wasn't getting paid, and the contact was regular enough for my home life to suffer.

Enough was enough. I told my boss that I was happy to receive texts or calls up until 7 pm, but anything after that would be picked up the next morning, as my phone would be turned off at that point.

He wasn't happy, and told me I should be reachable 24 hours a day, but I explained that working that late was having personal consequences for me. He still wasn't happy, but he agreed to ease off.

Implementing that boundary wasn't easy, especially as I love to just pick up the phone and help people whenever possible. I hated feeling like I was letting him down, but the wrath of my wife trumped my boss's disappointment. As an outsider, she could see the stress it was causing me, which was slowly invading our home. I had to do something, and I did. I am learning through experience what is good for me, and what isn't.

Steps to Build Strong Boundaries

Whenever somebody asks you to do something, what do you normally reply with? *Sure, I'll get straight on it. Of course. No problem.* Falling over yourself to help other people is a sign that you will drop whatever you have going on, things that may be very important to you: a plan you had, a job interview, work itself, or just taking a day to look after yourself. If you can't do what you need to do for you, how are you able to offer any energy back into the world?

There are steps you can take to build boundaries so strong, you will feel like a different person. This doesn't mean suddenly transforming into the most selfish person in the world; it's understanding that you have needs, too. You deserve to be happy, and feel safe.

The first step I always advise people to do when they want to build strong boundaries is to start small. You don't need to go in with guns blazing, announcing to people that you're no longer going to put up with their crap. Think about what bothers you the most, and start with that.

You can do this by being clear on what it is you want to change, both with others and yourself. You'll notice how strange it feels, almost like you're being pulled back to opening up that boundary space again. In those moments, remember why you're doing it, what your goal is, and how you can set strong boundaries without being unkind.

The second step is to *practice!* Speak in the mirror, write out what you want to say, and think about how you can execute it in a way that aligns with yourself. This gives you time to channel your boundaries through your caring nature.

Asserting Your Limits

The word "*assertive*" can sound harsh when you're just getting used to boundaries and applying them, but it's one that I want you to get used to. Assertiveness is actually a core communication skill, and I think it gets lost on many. It can sometimes be confused with rudeness, but I believe that's because it isn't being used correctly in many cases.

I believe the following tools will add an assertive angle to your character, allowing you to communicate your boundaries effectively, without causing offence in others.

Think about you first. Are you somebody who expresses their thoughts, or do you stay quiet? It might be worth reassessing how you communicate, so that when you need to assert your limits, you can do so properly.

Use your "I!" If you want to let people know how you're feeling, state it as "I don't agree" rather than "You're wrong."

Body Language. If you look confident, others will see you as such (plus you will feel it). Try not to hunch, stand a little taller, don't cross your arms, and practice eye contact. It all adds up to giving the other person the impression that you have clear boundaries, as well as limits.

Never Let Your Emotions Get the Better of You. It can be hard when faced with asserting your limits, but don't let anybody make you crumble. Keep your voice calm, breathe slowly, and remember to remain firm. It takes practice, but it will be worth it.

Somebody Pushing You? Lean In!

I know you will agree with me when I say the best way to react to somebody pushing your boundaries is to be as polite as you can; but never let that politeness cave in your boundary. In other words, you have to be firm, but you don't have to be rude. To snap back with rudeness would be to give the kind of reaction that shows that you allow others to dictate how you feel, a big no-no. You can *show 'em who's boss* by being a good boss! These four exercises will help you.

Remind yourself what all this is for. Go back to the start. You're looking for real change, and real change only comes when you change these parts of your life.

Reaffirm yourself. "No" is a complete sentence. You do not need to apologize, nor do you need to explain yourself.

Understand that you can't force somebody to listen. If they're trying hard to walk all over you, the chances are they're either used to doing that with everybody they meet, or they're used to doing it with you.

Accept that you won't please everybody. Not everybody will like your boundaries. This "new you" means they have to acknowledge they no longer get a free ride.

Chapter Eight

Discovering Once Lost Joy

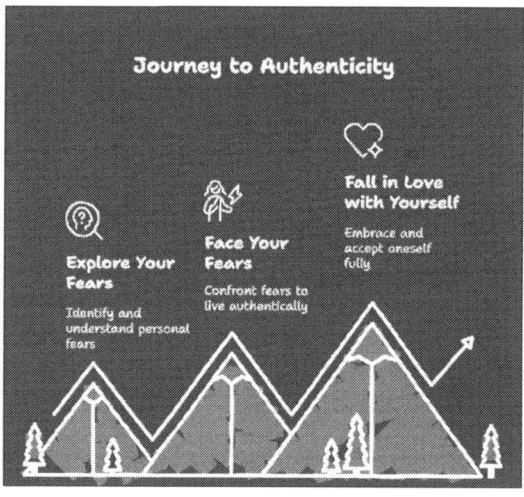

Joy does not simply happen to us. We have to choose joy and keep choosing it every day.

—Henri Nouwen

Henri's quote above needed a spot in this book, and I am so glad I found one. It felt good to insert it here and remind you that joy is only present when you are consciously aware of its existence. *If you deny the sun, you will never see the light.*

Choose joy every day, in every way you can, and I promise your heart will grow and be filled with love for yourself.

Reconnecting with joy is a little like learning to ride a bike after years of not owning one. It feels strange at first, but soon enough it will come flooding back to you.

Play and Healing: Hand in Hand

I used to live next door to a woman who had twin boys. They would spend so much time in the safety of their backyard, and I would frequently hear curious conversations between each other, squeals of joy, the odd tear here and there, but on the whole, contentment to be able to explore and play.

For me, it was a wonderful sound, but initially it felt odd to hear. I don't recall these memories in my own childhood. I wasn't encouraged to play, or be in any environment that encouraged it.

When we break down the act of playing, what really *is* it? If children are allowed to play, then they have automatic permission to express themselves. The environment in which they do so, like the twins, is typically safe. From play comes a strong sense of self. *I know what I know. I like what I like. I don't like what I don't like. This brings me joy. This makes me laugh. That makes me brave. I learn to share. Accept. Encourage. I learn how to handle stress.*

If play wasn't a part of your childhood, then you missed out on all the above. That's a tough pill to swallow, isn't it? Without the healing layers that play gave you, there are no layers readily available to you as an adult. Many would argue that this is the reason they *can't* heal, but there's no reason why you can't build those layers. Your inner child would definitely support me on this!

Be Creative to Engage

So what can you do to build those layers? Well, it *all starts* with a sprinkle of creativity. Before you dig out your glue sticks and glitter, though, I want you to think for a moment about what *really resonates with you* in the creative world. It can be getting completely messy with that glue and glitter! But it can also be singing. Joining a drama club. What about movement, like dance? Writing? Drawing? Painting? Clay modeling? When you start to unravel creativity, it will *never stop showing itself to you.*

I have three steps of advice that I want to share with you. They're small steps, but each one needs your attention and thought.

Step One: Think about what you wanted as a child, but were never given the space to have, then think about what you would need to do it now. If it was painting, for example, that list might include paints, brushes, canvas or watercolor paper, etc.

Step Two: Gather your supplies! If it's dance, create a playlist of songs that make you feel happy. If it's writing, get yourself to the nearest stationary shop and buy what you need.

Step Three: Start small. Going in with all the hope and anticipation in the world will more than likely spell disaster. Short-term success is *not* what we're after. Start, then listen to how your body feels. Try to engage mindfully in the moment.

These three steps are not specifically directed at finding your inner child, but they will by nature awaken them. If you practice and engage in creativity consistently, one day you will have that moment where you say, "Yes. I feel them with me." That can be where you both take off on creative adventures together!

Remember again what Nouwen said. *Choose joy.* When you learn to be creative, you learn to naturally shake off unnecessarily inhibitions. Even if that doesn't come as naturally as you'd hope, there *is* still hope.

Let Go of Inhibition

Do you ever feel something is holding you back, yet you can't quite figure out what? You can be told a thousand times to let go of your inhibitions, but you still might not recognize that this is what you're doing, until you sit down and really focus on it for the first time.

Inhibitions act like traps; but unlike most traps, these are ones you have the key to. It's not about what people think of you that's the problem, it's how *you perceive* what they think of you. People can think whatever they like (and often do), but it shouldn't affect how you act, what you want, and how you behave. As long as you aren't being overtly rude or scheming, you should be living your life free of the fear of judgment.

Letting go of inhibitions can prove successful if you follow my simple three-step plan.

Step One: Explore your fears. I need you to get specific and figure out what it is that scares you about being yourself without inhibition. Was there a time you didn't hold back and were judged? Who judged you? How did it make you feel? All inhibitions derive from fear, but they were created by *you*. This means you have the power to overturn them!

Step Two: Face your fears. I could write an entire book about facing your fears, but the main thing you need to know is to face everything, no matter how scary it might seem. If you can face your fears, your life will thank you for letting it be unapologetically authentic.

Step Three: Fall in love with yourself. I've spoken about self-love, but this is really the most actionable step you can take to let go of your inhibitions. Accept yourself for who you are. Know that you are a force of nature.

Our childhoods have such a lot to answer for, but inhibitions don't have to exist. They can be something you conquer; and if you do, like Michael, your outlook can change for good.

Case Study: Michael

As an adult, I thought being playful meant being immature. I grew out of playing very quickly. I had to. My parents didn't care for me "messing around" and I had to focus on homework, sports, and keeping the house in order. They expected so much of me, even at the age of ten. Soon enough, all my toys were packed away, even my LEGOs, which I loved.

I lost a huge part of my childhood saying a premature goodbye to getting to be playful. Even when I was playing basketball for my school team, practice at home wasn't fun. Hoop after hoop. Do better. Be better. Quit slacking.

I was at the park a while ago on a run, and there were some college kids shooting hoops at the court. The ball ran over toward me, so I picked it up and tossed it straight into the hoop. I got several cheers from them, and they asked me if I used to play. I said yes, and they asked if I could make up numbers for a 3-on-3 game. All I could hear was my father's voice, telling me to be better, but the looks on the kids' faces were full of hope and joy at the thought. So I said yes.

It was the best twenty minutes I have experienced in two decades. We shouted, we screeched, we passed, we cheered. It was the best time ever. It reminded me that I love basketball, even though I learned not to as a kid.

I then realized at that moment that it wasn't basketball that was the issue. It never was. My outlook changed, and I started looking at all the other things I stopped doing because I mistook my dread for criticism as hating them.

Creating a Life You Love

If the life you wanted was a house, and you had a pen and paper, how would you draw it? Would it have huge floor-to-ceiling windows? Might it have warm lighting in every room? Would it be in the middle of a city, or on the edge of a national park with great views? Would it be a large beach house or a small, cozy cottage? The choice is yours. The paper is blank, and the pen is in your hand.

It's the same for your actual life. It really is up to you how you create it. Most importantly, it has to represent you, what you want from it, what it has previously lacked, and all the enriching ways you can make it fulfilled.

Vision Boards and Long-Term Goals

To start visualizing that perfect life, you need to start from the beginning. I believe the strongest way to do that is through vision boards and setting goals. Also known as mood boards or action boards, vision boards are an opportunity for *anybody* to bring to life a representation of what they want their life to look like. Use cuttings from magazines, quotes, photos, illustrations, colors, words, anything that really builds what you're envisaging.

These boards inspire motivation, and they inspire people to aspire. That's the reason they are so effective *and* popular. Wouldn't it be great to have something you designed be the catalyst that pushes you toward your dreams? Visually, images are faster and easier for the brain to process, so there is higher value in pictures than text. Vision boards act as a powerful tool here.

You can build a vision board any way you choose, from creating a physical board on your wall at home or on a big piece of cardstock, or a digital one on your computer. The key is to see it every day, add to it if you need to, and value it. Seeing it before bed every night helps your vision board drift into your subconscious thoughts or dreams you may have, extending and deepening its meaning.

Vision boards are the initial long-term goals you create for yourself, and I know from experience that they work. When I made mine, it was based around physical fitness. I had motivational quotes, photos of people running or hiking, and colors of nature to help me think about being outdoors. I made sure to include a few bottles of water, too. The board drew me to take charge of my fitness, and I still run or walk most days now. You can see the same results, whatever they mean personally for you, if you give it a try.

The Eye of the Child

When healing momentarily feels heavy, those days can seem like the universe telling you to quit. I don't want you to do that. In fact, it's those kinds of days you need your childlike wonder the most. When you were a toddler learning to walk, you didn't try, fall down, and never walk again. You got up and kept trying.

If you look for it, life will always throw an excuse your way to stop. But we become what we look for. All I am asking you to do is look for the good. Look for the joy. Settle for what you're *really* worth, not what you've been programmed to *believe* you're worth.

Seeing life through a child's eyes means you see the simplicity. You don't search for complicated answers, because they only serve to slow you down. Immerse yourself in the world around you, and look for ways to shake up your routine. Say yes to new experiences, and be open to new hobbies. Change the way you behave, and the way you think will change with it.

Your life is made out of moments that shape you, and we all started off as children. Although your curiosity may have been stunted by the overwhelming and premature demand to grow up and experience trauma, it does not mean you lack the ability to be curious now.

When you need to, channel your inner child. Think about what they might want from the moment you're in. Look for things they would be in awe of. Love the little things.

Chapter Nine

Sustaining Emotional Freedom

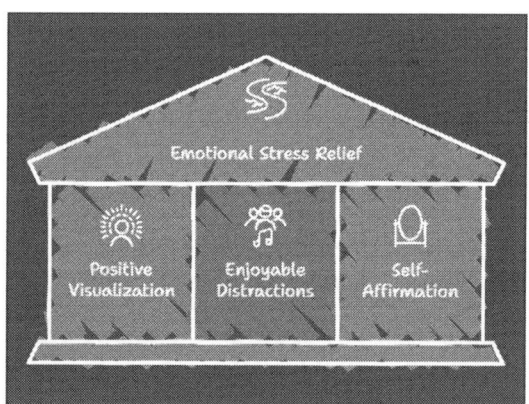

You wake up one morning, free from fear. You are in a place where you no longer react to what goes on around you. The decisions you make are wise, and you're aware of what you need to live not just better but consistently well.

Waking up like this means you have sustained emotional freedom, and although you may not be there yet, I have every confidence that you *will* be. The root of all emotional freedom is freedom of fear. Yes, being worried still may arise, but it's not letting the worry derail you that is key. If you can get to that point, you can avoid relapse.

Avoiding Relapse

What would life be without the odd wobble? *Relapse for you might look like:*

- *Retreating back into yourself*
- *Saying no when you need to say yes*
- *Saying yes when you ought to say no*
- *Holding back time and effort with your inner child*
- *Losing that spark you were regaining*
- *Refusing to believe you can heal*
- *Settling back into old habits*

It's signs like these that can let you know you're walking back into your past, the one place where familiarity trumped happiness. But there *is* beauty in healing.

The Daily Beauty of Healing

When you're not used to looking for the beautiful things, the beautiful things will never appear. I think of healing like making pastry by hand. First you add the flour to the bowl, then the butter, then the sugar. There comes that moment where you look inside the bowl at all these ingredients lumped together, and you know what you have to do next. You need to roll your sleeves up, wash your hands, and get stuck in. It all needs mixing, and it can get so messy that you think to yourself, "Whose idea was this?" Eventually, the flour, butter, and sugar begin to bind, and dough begins to form.

Now, the old you might look into that bowl, roll up your sleeves, wash your hands, and start. But the mess soon becomes too much, and it seems like a lot of hard work. So you quit. What you're left with is a bowl of goop that you can't use, bake, or eat.

Old patterns stop you from getting to the finish line. They prevent the process you're so desperate to see play out. If you want to heal, you need to roll your sleeves up every day and shape your life the way you want to shape that dough. If you can find beauty in healing, you will keep those old patterns or ways of life from returning.

When Old Patterns Come Knocking

Knock, knock. Who's there? Old patterns. Old patterns who? Old patterns who need to get the heck out of here!

No, there was no punchline, but there is a deliverable message here: *Old patterns have no room in your new life.* They will dampen the air, dim the lights, and fog the windows up in your new house of confidence and self-worth. Together, we cannot let that happen.

Recognizing old patterns is a powerful sign that you are changing from the inside out. But as the saying goes, old habits die hard, so don't take it personally. Life will do what it can to throw obstacles your way. This isn't personal, and should never be taken as such. These obstacles are also not an opportunity for you to incorrectly assume that life is pulling you back to your old habits. The recognition of an old habit comes from the recognition of an old feeling. This is where *you* come in. Notice:

- *The anxiety*
- *The dis-ease*
- *The depression*
- *The emotional retreat*
- *Lack of progression in your journey*
- *The shut down*
- *Progress stalling*
- *Fear creeping in*
- *Boundaries being encroached again*
- *Stress. Untold stress.*

- *Your inner child back in hiding*

So what do you do when you start to feel drawn back into the past version of you? Your recovery plan springs into action!

The Plan For Recovery

Recovery plans need to be specific in order for them to work. I want to keep it simple for that reason, but I need you to remember *three steps*. Missing one out may result in your old habits winning.

Step 1: Take a breath. Congratulations. You have successfully recognized your old self being different from the self you are trying to build. Take a moment to breathe and see the beauty in that.

Step 2: Ask yourself, *"How can I choose differently in this moment?"* Choosing what you've always chosen has proven not to work. This means you need to find a way to alter your path. Say to yourself things like:

- *I will not eat the unhealthy snack, because that is what I always do.*
- *I will still go out with my friends tonight, because the old me would have canceled.*
- *I will put my favorite song on and shake off these feelings.*
- *I will sit with the feeling of dis-ease, and tune into what my body and mind need.*
- *I will pick up my journal, because that's what makes me feel better.*

Step 3: Remind yourself that you have the power to shift every moment, whether good or bad. Knowing that the bad is bad and doesn't work, your only other choice for growth long-term is to choose the good.

What will work for you also worked for Jessica. Here's how.

Case Study: Jessica

All I can say is, thank goodness for my journal. Honestly, I bought one never thinking I would be writing a single word, but here I am nearly two years later, and on my fifth!

I listened to a podcast series about healing and finding your inner child. I'd be on the way to work, running errands, doing yard work, and I would have the podcast playing in my ears. It taught me so much, but the one thing that really stood out for me was how writing can be what carries you on your journey. I believe we all need an outlet to use every day, and I wasn't willing to try this journey of healing my inner child without finding what worked.

My journal is used twice a day. Once in the morning, I write down three things I want to achieve that day (no matter how small); and at the end of each day, I write down any worries, plus three things I am grateful for that day.

You have to be consistent. This is long-term. It's not a dip in, dip out activity. It doesn't work that way. The beauty is that you notice the difference even after the first few days. The mind feels lighter. Every now and then I have a thought dump on the days my head feels more chaotic than usual. And that's okay. I make my own rules, and as my mind clears, I make space for my inner child to come forward and spend time with me.

Compassion and Confidence

With one step comes another. Before you know it, you're not just standing up and moving an inch forward—you are walking the entire path!

I know what it can feel like to see such a long road ahead of you. When you can't see the destination, it's enough to quit the journey. But it's not about the destination. We all know what we want; to feel better, to live better, and to see the past for what it is—the past.

The *journey* is where we grow, discover, learn, cry, laugh, heal, reflect, forgive, trust, and love. *That's* where you put your energy. Soon enough, the destination will appear, and you will be ready for it when it does. Until then, any challenges you face should be met with two key things—compassion and confidence. Let's look at each of those subjects in more detail.

Compassion. You were taught in childhood that mistakes are bad, and never to make them. What you did *had* to be perfect, otherwise you would fail. Over time, that came to look like a refusal to even try, because of fear of not succeeding.

Do you know how damaging that is? Compassion is the start of you admitting that mistakes are par for the course in life. What's the worst that can *really* happen if you make a mistake? Be kind to yourself. Mistakes are how we find new ways to succeed.

Confidence. If you believe in yourself, that belief will turn into action. Action is necessary when faced with challenges, because you can't ignore what's in front of you. If it's difficult, switching off isn't going to give you the tools you need to face more. True confidence is being so okay with yourself that you don't see setbacks as problems.

Think about how any challenge can be solved with compassion and confidence, just like Iris.

Case Study: Iris

If you're reading this, it means I've gotten to a point where I have healed. I never thought I would get to write my own story. I didn't think healing was possible. You see people heal every day, but my life was so messy, it just felt like a train I missed.

I made the mistake of assuming that healing would happen to me with little to minimum input from *me. I passively waited, like I was waiting for a bus. Where was it? Check my watch. It was late. I got angry. Why was I being subjected to this delay?*

Then it dawned on me. I needed to heal, and I needed to be the one to do it. Nobody else was going to do it for me. And so, after a good week of crying because I had to put in work that felt overwhelming, I promised myself one thing; to take it one day at a time.

I had never utilized the power of time this way before, but each day I did one thing that made me feel better. Mostly this consisted of dancing, writing, walking, or tending to my vegetable plants (if I could take care of those, I could take care of me). Watching them grow and produce fruit based on how I treated them led me to realize that I could grow and produce courage if I did the same for myself.

I didn't plant myself in compost and water myself twice a day, but I did *do the other things. Soon enough, that fear became smaller, and I mean really small. Life felt balanced, and all because of the little changes I made along the way. This balance wasn't handed to me on a plate like I thought it would be. Instead, I provided it for myself. I knew I had to rely on myself, and so I did.*

This relationship I have with myself is only possible due to the time I give myself on a regular basis. I check in with myself, and I have gotten to know who I am underneath the fear and previous loss of identity.

A Balanced Life Begins With You

Anything you do regularly will become a solid part of your life, which affects how you function and respond. How about making sure that what you do *helps* you, rather than *hinders* you?

A healthy life is all about balance. You can find that in tuning in to the moment. We've talked about how important it is to be mindful, but you only really know, see, and feel the benefits if you practice often. Try these tips to help you out:

- Stand on the ground barefoot and close your eyes. Remain there for a few minutes, and feel part of something bigger than your trauma.

- Listen to the leaves on the trees shaking and rustling. Hear what is always around you.

- Chew your food with intent to taste, savor, and feel. Chew every last bite. Why rush what you put into your body?

I believe mindfulness isn't about living in the now, it's *being* in the now. And that being denotes balance. Soon enough, you will learn what it means to become your own anchor in times of need, and stress can become a manageable part of daily life.

Becoming Your Own Anchor

What do you think it means to become your own anchor? I don't want you to go out and buy yourself a new tugboat, but what I *do* want is to give you a chance to see anchoring as a concept you can live by each and every day.

Imagine you are experiencing a moment that has become overwhelming to you. You're in distress, and everything feels just *too much*. What do you do? The answer is to anchor. To connect and pin yourself down to your values, whatever goals you have, and focus in the moment on what you want, rather than what is happening.

Here are three techniques to help your self-ground during times of real stress.

Picture people you care about. Not just as a flash before you, but in real detail; their smile, their laugh, the way they support or love you, the memories you have together. Igniting the positive within you will be your body's way of counteracting the stress you feel.

Switch to something you love to hear or see. I *love* watching videos online of soldiers returning home after a tour of duty, if I feel like I need some time out. They remind me that there is love in the world, and that having people around you is so vital. What about you? A favorite band, song, video, show? If it works, do it for twenty minutes to really reduce the stress.

Say kind things to yourself. You know about affirmations, but this is more personal and in the moment. *I give myself too much of a hard time. It'll be okay, and this will pass. You're doing a great job today. I can choose happiness, and I will. You've got this.*

How surprising it can be when you respond positively to statements you offer yourself. We all need to do that from time to time, and it really does work.

Stress kills all emotional freedom, as Ava learned the hard way.

Case Study: Ava

My mind used to feel like a room where nothing could escape. Instead of letting go of the day, I would keep everything inside. It would build up and up and eventually it'd feel fit to burst. I wanted to scream, as I couldn't think straight or even breathe some days. My anxiety from my trauma grew, even when I didn't really notice. I didn't work on it, and I refused to believe it had become something that I couldn't control.

My anxiety was so high that it was all I ever thought about. I'd tune into my racing heart and become worried it was going to just fail on me. I'd worry about not being able to fall asleep that night, and then be even more tired the next day. I'd worry about dying early and leaving my son without a mother.

It was too much, until I turned into it and understood what I had been unintentionally watering my whole life. That's the truth. We water what we pay attention to, and there's no freedom in watering fear. Emotional freedom became a conscious belief I could work through at that point.

Accepting that I live with anxiety meant I had to let go of the frustration of it being alive within me. To shrink it, I had to lose the idea that I was unworthy, but without trying to control every aspect of my life.

Let go. Choose freedom. The moment you do, you will become addicted to it. Over time, you'll be able to do what you previously would have struggled with. I guarantee the hardest part is taking that first step. The rest will make you think, "I did it."

Chapter Ten

Transforming Pain Into Power

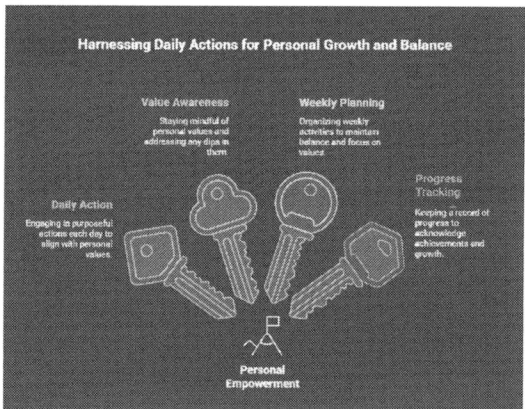

Pain and power are different currencies. They both hold value, but only one has a longstanding positive effect on you.

We cannot avoid pain (believe me, I've tried!). It is inevitable, one of the things we all have in common. Instead of holding onto it, we need to transform it into power, so that we can hold the proper currency in our hands. Power is much easier to spend and reap the rewards from.

Your pain from your childhood has been your currency for all this time. No wonder you haven't been able to spend it. Challenging childhoods can be a gift that transforms the way we think, act, behave, and feel about ourselves.

The Gift of a Challenging Childhood

It's hard to find meaning in pain. It's hard to find the prize in a challenge that leaves you traumatized. The trauma was never meant to be your whole book, it was just supposed to be a chapter. The rest of your book is overcoming it and figuring out who you are *after* it.

Adversity is all around us, and I believe we all experience it at some point in our lives. If we start off with a strong, happy, and healthy childhood, that adversity is likely to be dealt with in a much more regulated fashion. If it's at the *start* of your life—well, those are weak foundations on which to build anything meaningful.

The gift of weak foundations is that you can always make them stronger, and that's where you agreed to embark on the journey of finding your inner child. The inner child is the part of you that became neglected when you needed to survive. You had to push it aside to fall in line, to fit in, and to find the version of yourself they needed you to be. And now, all of that has gone. As an adult, *you* call the shots. *You* make the choices. *You* decide what's right for you. How do I know this? Because I used to be you.

Helping Others Heal

When I was little, the first warning sign of a challenging childhood I had was a feeling of knots in my stomach. Bedtime would arrive and I would feel butterflies of unease. I'd try and fall asleep, but much of the time it didn't come naturally to me. I'd watch my mother—a stay-at-home parent—flit so effortlessly during the day between caring for me and tending to the housework.

Her demeanor would alter the moment she heard my father come home from work. Her back would straighten, her smile would fade, and her foot would start to tap. She would busy herself, and as time went on, I noticed her faded character shift onto me, too. I didn't know at the time that it had a name. I just knew I felt unwell. Over time, I watched my father shout, throw things, criticize, mock, isolate, ignore, dismiss, and make me smaller. The irony of growing up, right? A time you're supposed to grow, and be a bigger presence in the world, was the time I shrank.

My journey into adulthood left me feeling like somebody who wasn't wanted. I felt in the way at home, with no means to move out. My mom tried to tell me how much my dad loved me, but I believe the single biggest mistake you can make is to teach a child that this treatment is love. I learned to tap into therapy, to understand the sheer scale of my childhood dysregulation. It opened a can of worms that was both necessary and messy, but it helped me see the whole picture.

I lost my innocence from an early age because I had to learn how to survive. I didn't know what it was like to play without snide comments about my choice of play, or how I should be liking other pastimes or hobbies instead. I learned not to like what I liked, and to pretend to like what I didn't. I also learned to people-please. If my dad needed something, I'd jump at the chance to help. I wanted him to love me, notice me, validate me. Whenever he requested I did more to help around the house as I got older, I'd cook dinner. He would not eat it. Too many onions. Too spicy. The potatoes were soggy. I'd watch him push the food around the plate like a teething toddler.

Every day, all my life, I lived inauthentically. I lost the part of me that radiated joy. I realized it was taken from me because my light was brighter than his, and this wasn't acceptable. Over time, I learned that contact with my father was detrimental to my mental, emotional and, in turn, physical health. I decided, "No more." Over the next *five years,* I learned more about myself and life than the previous 35. I'm still learning now, but I believe most of the heavy groundwork is done.

I wish I had learned sooner and gotten more of my life back, but I truly don't believe you can start to heal unless you're fully awakened to the trauma you're healing from. The pain feels enormous at first, at least it did for me. How can a man who is supposed to be my father neglect me? How can he live literally ten minutes from my house and not want to see me, or find out why I went with no contact? How can somebody morally be okay with hurting other people this way? Until one day, I understood. It wasn't me. It was him.

I've spent the last several years rebuilding my life: my confidence, my self-worth, my self-belief, my hobbies, what brings me joy, what I like to eat, what I like to read, even singing! My son was born, and I got on the floor with him and smiled, laughed, responded, and absorbed *every part* of his childhood. He is bright, emotionally intelligent, funny, strong, resilient, and playful. He is allowed to be himself, and his home is a safe place.

My childhood was challenging, but in a way I've become the person I am today because I had to learn what all of that meant. And now, I can finally live *authentically.* I want to offer you exercises to help you align your actions with your values. It seems the most appropriate way to usher you to the final section of this book.

Living Authentically

Everything begins with alignment. Your authentic self is who you are, why you are, and how you continue to live it through your purpose. You can't just write your values down on a piece of paper and then immediately start living by them. They have to be effective. They need shape, color, depth. They need *you*.

Here are 15 values to help you think about what matters to you. I've based them on *very* broad living experiences, but you can add on as many for yourself as you want to.

- Acceptance
- Achievement
- Balance
- Compassion
- Courage
- Creativity
- Family
- Forgiveness
- Fun
- Gratitude
- Health
- Mindfulness
- Power
- Self-acceptance
- Truth

When reading those, what would you rate them out of ten, with ten being the most valuable possible in your life, and zero being nothing at all? Now, how do you align your actions with those values?

Actioning your values means being conscious that they exist and to live by them with intent. The following will help you with both:

Action every day with awareness. Keep what you value in the forefront of your mind, and respond to the world around you as if you were honoring them. If family means a lot to you, keep in touch with the ones you love and trust. Meet regularly. Support them. If it's health, tap into what health means for you, and how you can keep your mental and physical health in good shape and balance. Be aware of what you need when you need it, and when to rest.

Keep a note of your values, and know when they're dipping for you. If they are, pick two to work on in the morning. Text that friend. Ground yourself. Meditate. Do something creative. Bring yourself back to that value.

Plan your week with your values in mind. If you are busy with work, find time to breathe among the chaos. Go for a lunchtime walk. Take in nature. *Activate* your power.

Keep a diary of your progress. Sometimes, the only way we can see how far we have come is to look back on something tangible. That way, we can't talk ourselves out of success.

In case you have never been told, *I believe in you, and I am proud of you.*

Conclusion

A Life Reclaimed

Conclusions indicate the end of something. They mark ways in which I, the author, wrap up all I've written and present it to you with a little bow. *I now turn things over to you. It's your turn. Go make your life amazing!* You close the book, having taken your precious time reading it (for which I am endlessly thankful for), and what?

I need you to know one vital piece of information: This book was not your journey. It had a beginning, a middle, and an end, but it wasn't your story. It's likely you've amassed a great deal of information as you went from chapter to chapter, and I've no doubt you have a few goals in your mind; how to start loving yourself more, forgiving not just others for inner peace, but yourself too, and where your boundaries can start being implemented (and kept).

Journeys to heal one's inner child come with the revisiting of new thoughts in order to create new habits. It *is* a legitimate challenge to leave everything you've ever known to be true and familiar, and turn to the unknown and yet unexplored. This is not a time to fear, however; it is a time to be excited. Every day, droves of people have that breakthrough moment. They've pushed past the barrier that's kept their comfort zone small, and they have reached out to their inner child successfully. Your breakthrough moment is out there. It is going to happen for you.

They say *that what doesn't kill you makes you stronger*, but I'm not a huge fan of that phrase. We shouldn't be forced to put a positive spin on the worst things that happen in our lives. That person is hurting. They feel lost and scared. They wonder if they will ever know true joy again. I know you probably don't feel that strong half the time, and to be assumed you are because you lived through trauma and lost sight of your inner child is belittling of you and your experiences.

I believe in the gift of healing, for all those who embark on the journey. There is not a straight line from pain to perfect. If it was, we would all walk it with ease, and we'd all be reaching our dreams within days. Healing involves taking two steps forward and one step back. One the days you step back, step back with the knowledge that your worth and strength to succeed are carrying you forward.

On the days you feel lost, offer yourself some much needed compassion. Work through your thoughts with your journal, or with your new reframing tools. Be as kind to yourself as you have been to everybody else you know, because that's the one thing that's been lacking with you.

The inner child is a part of you that never left. Even when you forgot they were there, they've remained by your side. Learning how to reach them and hold their hand proves that anything is possible, and your healing will be all the more enriched for that.

Healing is lifelong. One day you will wake up with a corner turned, and you will notice the air around you feeling lighter. You will pause to watch a moment of nature, and you will be drawn to the stillness of peace, rather than the previously familiar triggering pain of trauma. And that's when you will finally know.

You've made it.

If you have found this "Healing Your Inner Child" guide beneficial, please share your experience by leaving a comment on the book's Amazon page.

With peace and gratitude, Avery

Please Leave A Review

Did you enjoy the book?

I would be deeply grateful if you could leave a review. Reviews are so important for authors and help others discover this book. Your feedback truly makes a difference.

Thank you for your support!

Please leave a review. I really appreciate it.

Click or Scan the QR Code. Thank you!

References

Raypole, C. (2020, June 26). Finding and getting to know your inner child. Healthline. https://www.healthline.com/health/inner-child

joy. (2023, January 10). Integrative Psychotherapy & Trauma Treatment. Integrative Psychotherapy & Trauma Treatment. https://integrativepsych.co/new-blog/2023/5/2/feel-the-feelings

Ackerman, C. (2017, June 18). 19 narrative therapy techniques, interventions + worksheets. PositivePsychology.com. https://positivepsychology.com/narrative-therapy/

How to Create a "Safe Space" Anyplace. (n.d.). VerywellMind. https://www.verywellmind.com/how-and-why-you-should-create-a-safe-space-for-yourself-3144981

Harvard Health Publishing. (2021, February 12). 4 ways to boost your self-compassion. Harvard Health; Harvard Health. https://www.health.harvard.edu/mental-health/4-ways-to-boost-your-self-compassion

Johns Hopkins Medicine. (2019). *Forgiveness: Your Health Depends on It*. Johns Hopkins Medicine. https://www.hopkinsmedicine.org/health/wellness-and-prevention/forgiveness-your-health-depends-on-it

Gupta, S. (2023, June 20). *What Does the Term "Emotional Baggage" Mean?* Verywell Mind. https://www.verywellmind.com/emotional-baggage-symptoms-causes-and-coping-strategies-6742778

10 Common Patterns Seen in Unresolved Relational Trauma. (2023). Psychology Today. https://www.psychologytoday.com/gb/blog/understanding-ptsd/202308/10-common-patterns-seen-in-unresolved-relational-trauma

Ishler, J. (2021, September 16). *Are You Carrying "Emotional Baggage" Here's How to Break Free*. Healthline. https://www.healthline.com/health/mind-body/how-to-release-emotional-baggage-and-the-tension-that-goes-with-it

Mayo Clinic Staff. (2022, November 22). *Forgiveness: Letting go of grudges and bitterness*. Mayo Clinic. https://www.mayoclinic.org/healthy-lifestyle/adult-health/in-depth/forgiveness/art-20047692

Adverse Childhood Experiences and its life long consequences | Other | the In Mind blog | In-Mind. (2024). In-Mind.org. https://in-mind.org/blog/post/adverse-childhood-experiences-and-its-lifelong-consequences?gad_source=1&gclid=Cj0KCQiAu8W6BhC-ARIsACEQoDD72CU_srMnHzINH3vMb9ixenQ0RbF0EA_a_f7lbpxU_E4lr6PuKhkaAs4-EALw_wcB

What is Reparenting and How to Begin. (2019, July 2). The Holistic Psychologist. https://theholisticpsychologist.com/what-is-reparenting-and-how-to-begin/

Copley, L. (2024, March 29). *Reparenting: Seeking Healing for Your Inner Child*. PositivePsychology.com. https://positivepsychology.com/reparenting/#what-is-reparenting

Want to raise strong, resilient kids? Create "nurturing routines," says parenting expert—here's how. (2022, September 25). CNBC.https://www.cnbc.com/2022/09/24/how-to-raise-resilient-kids-by-developing-their-brains-with-nurturing-routines-parenting-expert.html

Cooks-Campbell, A. (2022, May 26). What self-love truly means and ways to cultivate it. Betterup.https://www.betterup.com/blog/self-love

How to regulate your nervous system? Try these 13techniques. (n.d.). Calm Blog.https://www.calm.com/blog/how-to-regulate-nervous-system

Breathing Exercises for Anxiety. (n.d.). Priory.https://www.priorygroup.com/blog/breathing-exercises-for-anxiety

Progressive Muscle Relaxation - Whole Health Library.(n.d.). Www.va.gov.https://www.va.gov/WHOLEHEALTHLIBRARY/tools/progressive-muscle-relaxation.asp

Selva, J. (2017, June 14). Shame Resilience Theory: Howto Respond to Feelings of Shame. PositivePsychology.com.https://positivepsychology.com/shame-resilience-theory/

The Speaker Lab. (2024, June 23). 12 Simple Exercises toBuild Confidence In Any Situation. The Speaker Lab.https://thespeakerlab.com/blog/confidence-building-exercises/

FrancescaLehrell. (2024, June 4). 5 Powerful Ways ToSilence Your Inner Critic - Been There. Been There.https://beenthereapp.com/5-powerful-ways-to-silence-your-inner-critic/?gad_source=1&gclid=CjwKCAiA6t-6BhA3EiwAltRFGBCS7oI18ZvgO3MjT4Bpioe gyIn8fyMB_331EmJOswsrlGAfLLZnHRoCDacQAvD_BwE

Stepping Out of Social Anxiety. (n.d.).https://www.cci.health.wa.gov.au/~/media/CCI/Consumer-Modules/Stepping-out-of-Social-Anxiety/Stepping-out-of-Social-Anxiety---Module-8---Challenging-Core-Beliefs.pdf

How to Rewrite Your Past Narrative | Psychology Today United Kingdom. (n.d.). Www.psychologytoday.com. Retrieved December 14, 2022,from https://www.psychologytoday.com/gb/blog/quantum-leaps/201907/how-rewrite-your-past-narrative

Therapy, H. (2019, June 25). 12 Signs You Lack Healthy Boundaries (and Why You Need Them) - Harley TherapyTM Blog. Harley TherapyTMBlog. https://www.harleytherapy.co.uk/counselling/healthy-boundaries.htm

5 Ways Childhood Trauma Affects Relationship Boundaries.(2023). Psychology Today. https://www.psychologytoday.com/gb/blog/flipping-out/202302/5-ways-childhood-trauma-affects-relationship-boundaries

Brooten-Brooks, M. C. (2022, January 24). How to SetHealthy Boundaries. Verywell Health.https://www.verywellhealth.com/setting-boundaries-5208802

Kove, R. (2012, May 17). How to Lose Your Inhibitions: 11 Ways to Be Less Self-Conscious. WikiHow. https://www.wikihow.com/Lose-Your-Inhibitions

Carla. (2021). When You Fall Into Old Habits | IntuitionContinuum. Intuition continuum.com. https://www.intuitioncontinuum.com/falling-into-old-habits/

Mayo Clinic . (2020, May 29). *Being assertive: Reducestress, communicate better*. Mayo Clinic.https://www.mayoclinic.org/healthy-lifestyle/stress-management/in-depth/assertive/art-20044644

Hailey, L. (2024, April 19). *How to set boundaries: 5ways to draw the line politely*. Science of People.https://www.scienceofpeople.com/how-to-set-boundaries/

Team, O. (2013, January 21). *How to Develop EmotionalFreedom - North Brisbane Psychologists*. North Brisbane Psychologists. https://northbrisbanepsychologists.com.au/emotional-freedom/

play scotland. (2023). *The Power of Play*. Play Scotland.https://www.playscotland.org/learn/what-is-play/the-power-of-play/

Doherty, L. (n.d.). *The science behind vision boards*. TheMotivation Clinic.https://www.themotivationclinic.co.uk/blog/blog-post-title-three-grwe9

Selma. (2023, September 10). *Rediscovering Life's MagicThrough Childlike Wonder ⋆ The Blue Brain T*. The Blue BrainTeacher.https://thebluebrainteacher.com/rediscovering-lifes-magic-through-childlike-wonder/

Shy. (2023, October 27). *Becoming Your Own Anchor inResponse to Trauma*. Blue Anchor Psych.https://www.blueanchorpsychology.com/post/becoming-your-own-anchor-in-response-to-trauma

Inner Child Wounds: 16 Signs & How to Heal Them.(n.d.). WikiHow. https://www.wikihow.com/Inner-Child-Wounds

100 + Meditation Statistics 2024: How Many PeopleMeditate Worldwide? (n.d.). Www.yogavidyaschool.com.https://www.yogavidyaschool.com/blog/meditation-statistics

Benefits of Journaling: The Science and Philosophy Behind Keeping a Diary. (n.d.). Intelligent Change.https://www.intelligentchange.com/blogs/read/benefits-of-journaling

Psychologies. (2022, March 17). *Non-dominant handwriting therapy.* Psychologies.https://www.psychologies.co.uk/non-dominant-hand-writing-therapy/

Exercises for defining and living your values. (n.d.). My Best Self 101.https://www.mybestself101.org/values-exercises

Printed in Great Britain
by Amazon

e3bd5991-4194-4099-ba50-e8815d19f54aR01